I too have a dream

When I awoke in the morning to feel the sun on my face,
I awoke from a dream that one day the children of our cultures will
live in peace.
That the questions they ask will be of innocence and joy not of pain.

> *I dreamed*

> *that one will not see the eyes of a child old before their time with*
> *the experience of prejudice and the confusion that brings*
> *that parents will not have to experience anger and the pain of*
> *   innocence shattered as they try to explain why*
> *that young people of both cultures would be able to meet and*
> *socialise freely, that no more would our young be turned from*
> *the doors and refused entry "you are not welcome here"*

> *I dreamed*

> *that the old would receive the respect of their age*
> *of equality, no more to see the pain on people's faces*
> *no longer to experience exclusion and insults, to live without*
> *fear and caution*
> *of welcome in society and the freedom to live as people wish*
> *where the laws will be just.*

> *I dreamed*

> *of my church, it was aware of my pain, it held out its arms to*
> *embrace me, to walk with me.*

I awoke in the morning to feel the sun on my face and so for now,
hope still lives.
As I rise to meet the day I wonder will this be the day that my dream
shall live?

Cathleen McDonagh

Published by the Parish of the Travelling People 2000.

St Laurence House,
6 New Cabra Road
Phibsborough
Dublin 7

Tel: 01 8388874
Fax: 01 8388901
e-mail: partravs@iol.ie

First edition May 2000
Second edition with updated statistics August 2000

Design and production: Pat Pidgeon

All photographs are copyright Dan O'Connell C.M. except pages 46, 47, 64, 127 and 147 Derek Speirs/Report, pages 10, 71 and 87 John McElroy, page 64 Cumann na Piobairi and page 178 Michael McSweeney

Printing: Printwell 10-11 Richmond Street, Dublin 1 tel: 01 8550873

ISBN No. 0 9521120 7 8

Acknowledgements

We would like to thank all who contributed to the book "Do You Know Us At All?" which was edited by John Hyland and was so successful, but which is now out of print. "Do you know us at all?" was the inspiration behind this book and we are very grateful to all the contributors especially those who kindly agreed to write new articles or to be interviewed for the purpose of compiling this book and also to the new contributors.

We offer our special thanks to all the parish staff, especially to Tammy Kiely and Melissa Stokes, and also John Donne who were so patient and persevering in writing out the long – taped interviews which formed the basis of some of the articles. Thanks also to Anne Hayden and Jackie Kavanagh for their typing up of the manuscript and to Anne O'Brien and Don O'Callaghan for help with the text. Finally, we extend our gratitude to those involved in the Citizen Traveller Campaign for the use of their materials and to Pavee Point for permission to draw on their definitions in compiling our own Glossary.

Contents

PART I – WHO ARE THE TRAVELLING PEOPLE?

Culture and Ethnicity

Traveller Spirituality

PART 11 – CHALLENGES FROM THE TRAVELLER COMMUNITY

Accommodation

Foreword by President McAleese

I am delighted to welcome this book produced by the Parish of the Travelling People who do such pioneering and valuable work on behalf of all the members of the Traveller Community.

This publication is of major importance at a time of such societal and economic change in Ireland. If we are to release our full potential and talents as a people we cannot afford to marginalise or exclude any individual in our society. It is important that each of us embrace and promote understanding and respect for group diversity and that we all cherish rather than shun differences in culture, creed and tradition. Such an understanding helps to avoid the pitfall of focusing negatively on minorities as somehow not conforming to our personal or group norms – and to recognise instead that all groups within society have their own unique characteristics – each adding its own colour, richness and distinctiveness to the mosaic that is the complex landscape of society. The Traveller Community have an especially rich cultural heritage which can only enhance and enrich our society

As we celebrate the momentous developments in Northern Ireland in recent times, it is worth reflecting on the factors that have made this progress possible and their relevance to creating a tolerant and respectful society for all the peoples of this island. It could not have happened at all if there had not been people on each side who were willing to listen to the other – to their stories, perceptions, fears and expectations.

To overcome the myths, prejudices and labelling that had been handed down as unshakeable truths, is to listen and to slowly grow in understanding, to discover the awesome power that can be harnessed when different traditions embrace each other widely and warmly. The journey towards joyful acceptance is still incomplete as many can testify. But from that experience and from endeavours such as this book there are lessons we can learn in considering how best we can embrace and include all members of our society in this new Millennium.

We enter this new Millennium with a level of prosperity of which previous generations could only have dreamed and with a real responsibility to use those opportunities to create a humanly decent and inclusive society – for our children and our older people, our homeless, our refugees, our Traveller and settled communities alike.

I warmly commend all those involved in compiling this book and wish you every success.

Guím rath agus séan ar bhur gcuid oibre.

Mary McAleese
President

Preface

The focus of this book is an exploration of Traveller culture with a view to promoting an understanding of Travellers as full and equal citizens of Ireland with their own culture and identity. We, in the Parish of the Travelling People, invite you the reader to enter into the richness and diversity of a people, without generalising, while at the same time discovering the overall collective identity of the Traveller community. We hope through this publication to highlight the issues within Irish society that deeply impact on and adversely affect Travellers' lives.

Part One of the book begins by exploring the concept of culture in general, focusing on the origins of the Traveller community and moving into aspects of our cultural expression such as ethnicity, nomadism, family, spirituality and customs.

Part Two highlights the basic human rights that are denied to members of the Traveller Community especially in regard to accommodation, health care and education. This section also deals with the bitter experience of prejudice that all Travellers have to contend with on a daily basis within Irish society.

The Conclusion entitled *"Challenges to Irish Society"*, in drawing together the central themes and issues of the book, faces us with the challenge to make a choice for a society where egalitarianism, (as opposed to individualism) and respect for cultural diversity are the underlying values that compel us not to rest until Travellers' rights as full citizens are realised.

We believe that central to overcoming ignorance and fear is dialogue between Traveller and settled, dialogue that is informed by truth. We need to create space to share our stories and experience and in doing so, we come to embrace the truth of ourselves and of others. It is only then that we can make real progress towards achieving an Irish society where all citizens are recognised and treated as equals.

We ask you to be open to the challenges posed by a people who are striving and seeking to have their identity and human rights acknowledged and respected. We ask no more than what settled people often take for granted. We ask no more or less than what our shared humanity demands.

You will come to know the truth,
And the truth will set you free. Jn-8: 32.

Cathleen McDonagh

Part 1

Who are the Travelling People?

Aspects of Traveller Culture

An insight into a commu
its faith and its cultu

What is culture?

Delores O'Sullivan

I'm Australian which means that I can speak as being from a different culture. It is my opinion that the Irish culture and the Australian culture are very similar. I belong to the Sisters of the Holy Spirit and we are spread throughout the world. The Sisters come from different cultures. We always live inter-culturally, at present where I am there is a German, a Pole, four Irish and myself. Culture is continually changing. What I'm going to say about culture is mostly common sense, but because we are so immersed in our own culture we are not aware of it.

Anthropologists observe people and search out the patterns in everything they do. Then anthropologists are able to arrange these patterns in an orderly way to assist people in understanding themselves. The classic definition of culture is the following:

"Culture donates a historically transmitted pattern of meaning, embodied in symbols by means of which men and women communicate, perpetuate and develop their knowledge about and their attitude to life."

Culture – sharing ideas

What defines culture is the set of ideas that a particular group of people have in common. These ideas produce behaviour, i.e. people 'do' something as a result of the way they think and believe and from such behaviour we see results. The results are material, for example style of houses, clothes, personal jewellery, (in short anything that is made) and, non-material for example in terms of their style of singing or playing music, how a particular group speak and how they interact with each other. It is in the context of the non-material realm that we encounter rituals, symbols, myths, and religion that give meaning to a people's society and their life.

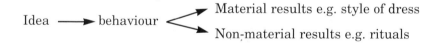

Idea ⟶ behaviour

Material results e.g. style of dress

Non-material results e.g. rituals

Culture – learning how to behave

In terms of culture it is ideas that are passed on not the actual behaviour. Culture is very important because it determines the manner in which society adapts itself to the environment. The needs are determined by the environment but the way in which people adapt to these needs is determined by their culture and by the historic experiences of the group. *We don't inherit behaviour patterns from our parents, we learn them.* When a child is born, it doesn't know love or hate, it learns to love and to hate. Children learn how to interact with people and how to express prejudices towards other cultures, e.g. settled children from a very young age learn to call Travellers "knackers" and Traveller children learn to be wary of settled people and not to socialise outside their own community.

Human beings cannot learn outside of a culture. Children who have been brought up by animals had no speech and their way of walking was not human, it was learned from animals. Although you have the capacity (i.e. the organs etc.) to speak a language, you don't automatically learn it, you have to learn how to speak from other humans around you. The child learns by observing, watching, listening and practising what they see going on in their culture. For example, different cultures have different ways of greeting; bow, shake hands, smile, wink, hug, kiss cheeks. Therefore, the way that we do things is the shared way of the group to which we belong and each person within the group has a similar pattern.

Culture – following a common map

A person's own ideas don't become part of the culture unless everybody shares the idea. For centuries slavery was accepted as a part of life. Nowadays, if a person thought slavery was acceptable or even desirable, most people would object. Slavery is no longer a shared idea of societies. Culture is like a shared map, a mental map that people have which indicates to them how they are going to fit into society. It doesn't give all the details of how to achieve this, but it does give the main patterns to be followed. Each individual will have a personal interpretation of how to follow the pattern and this gives a person security. People outside a group often become confused at small differences in behaviour. Travellers for example, find it very hard to understand why settled people do not openly grieve at a funeral, because for Travellers this would mean that they didn't really love the person. On the other hand, when settled people see Travellers expressing their grief openly and oftentimes loudly, they find it strange and confusing. These differences in ideas and behaviour are manifesting themselves all the time. When I go to a funeral in another culture I'm not sure if I should meet the relatives before or after the prayers are said, so I watch what everyone else is doing and I follow suit. In this way I demonstrate the correct behaviour in that particular culture.

Culture can't exist on its own. Culture only exists in people. Society wouldn't survive without culture, as culture dictates how society operates, from securing food, to deciding who does what in society. A society is a group of people who share a common culture and language and are sufficiently different from surrounding groups to form a distinct group e.g. the Traveller community in Ireland is a distinct cultural group with its own shared values, customs, language and way of life.

Cultural survival in times of change

A few years ago I was living in the Northern Territory with the Aborigines, who have a lot in common with Irish Travellers. In this region, the dominant non-Aborigine culture is taking over. It was interesting to see what still remained of Aboriginal culture. In traditional times anyone who didn't keep the laws was banished for a time. Now, although they are all living in houses, they still take lads who are acting up to a nearby island, where they are to stay for a certain amount of time. It is interesting to see that, in spite of all the changes, some key elements of their traditional culture remains. When both the idea and the behaviour remain close together the society is stable. Too many changes make the society disintegrate. For example, the government policies (both past and present) in regard to Traveller accommodation try to force Travellers to resettle i.e. "settle down" which puts a huge strain on one of the defining features of Traveller identity i.e. nomadism. These policies have enormously adverse effects on the survival of the Traveller way of life. This of course leads to anarchy.

Cultural superiority

Is one culture superior to another? What do we mean by progress? If we are talking about technology and advance we draw a triangle, at the top of the apex we would have the urban 'civilised' people and at the bottom the 'primitive' people because these people are not as technologically advanced. Nevertheless, if we were ranking societies on the basis of social relationships, 'primitive' people would be at the top and 'civilised' people would be at the bottom. Who decides which is the better culture? The Aborigines were technologically the least advanced but they had the most elaborate social system. They know about categories of family and who all their relatives are, in precisely the same way as Travellers in Ireland do. Aborigines have different names for their relationships and the children know these. It is a very elaborate system and you would say that in terms of relationship Aborigines are extremely advanced. Therefore, what would be considered primitive and what is considered civilised are open to question. It is easy for any person to believe that their culture is better than somebody else's culture. In reality this is not the case, as it is only one person's opinion and this opinion can very quickly become the basis of racism. To a person from another culture, their reasons for acting in a certain way can be as logical as our reasons for doing it differently. Buying is something we all do, for some it is impersonal - you go in, you pay the money, for others it is a social event, person to person you bargain with one another and market days are for getting together.

What constitutes culture?

Diagram of a Culture

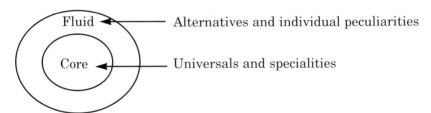

Our diagram shows two zones within culture. The fluid zone holds those things that can easily change. Do you add milk to the mug before pouring tea or do you pour the tea, then milk or is the milk first added to the teapot? This is referred to as an individual peculiarity. Alternatives, also in the fluid zone are traits shared by individuals but not necessarily shared by all the group, i.e. Irish people could be Catholic, Protestant, Jewish, Muslim or Atheist. To take the example of physical exercise for many that may mean Gaelic Football or Soccer for others it may mean walking or aerobics or cycling etc.

The second zone is the core zone. This zone is the most resistant to change and deals with universals. Universals are ideas, habits and emotions strongly held by members of the group and these universals may be held in common with other cultures. These ideas may include rights of people to, proper accommodation, access to education, sufficient food for survival, proper health care etc. Among universals are our language, our dress, our social relations, our values, beliefs and worldviews.

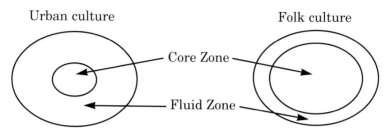

In urban culture the core zone is very small. We don't have an enormous amount in common. The larger area is where people do the things they like, whereas in the folk culture there is a large area of core zone, and the number of differences is small. Within the concept of the core zone and the fluid zone we can place in each, aspects of our culture that we are familiar with. It is when we can separate the things that belong to the core zone and those that belong to the fluid zone that we can gain a deeper understanding of a culture.

If we were to take the concept of nomadism in Traveller culture, we can place this within the core zone. There is more to the concept of nomadism than travel. Nomadism is a way of perceiving and engaging in life. This belongs to the core zone of culture and the values that it holds are also central to the core beliefs of a people. The fluid zone of Traveller culture on the other hand, holds things that can change easily, changing fashions in the style of dress, the mode of transport from the horse drawn car to the motor car. Modes of transport have changed with the times but the concept that is behind travel has remained the same. The core zone holds the concept, which is ingrained in people's psyche.

Understanding other cultures

We are conditioned by culture to think and act the way we do and we think it is normal. If we go to another culture we sometimes feel lost. We talk about experiencing culture shock when we don't know how to act in another culture. Sometimes we can't understand why people are laughing or behaving in a certain way. Naturally, we feel disoriented. If we stay long enough however, we can understand some of the patterns and can live in a cross – cultural situation. People within the culture, would talk about things their way and we, looking in from the outside see it differently or think there is a different explanation. There are different people who in their own culture have a deeper understanding of their culture.

Conclusion

Culture

◆ provides symbols, rituals and myths that give meaning to life

◆ teaches cultural ideals for living

◆ structures society

◆ teaches the appropriate manner of meeting biological needs

◆ sets standard patterns of behaviour that are acceptable

◆ influences assumptions, motivations, values, thought patterns

◆ teaches skills for communicating – language etc.

Origins of the Travelling People

Michael McDonagh

Introduction

I feel it is very important when people talk of Travellers to look at their origins, because this will not only condition the way people think about Travellers but will also dictate what kind of services they will provide and the way these services will be delivered. It's important to show the origins of Travellers so that people's mind-sets and way of thinking changes. No longer is it acceptable to say that Travellers were settled people and therefore it's perfectly alright to resettle or re-assimilate them. Now you must look at Travellers as having an identity and culture to be celebrated and resourced.

Descendants of the landless famine victims

There are many theories about the origin of the Travelling people. The most common one which has much support from the settled community is that Irish Travellers are the descendants of the people who lost their land at the time of the Famine. It suits a lot of people to say that Travellers originate from this point in history because then it allows people to believe that prior to this, Travellers would have been settled people. Hence, Travellers appearing in 1840 would mean that they were in some way "failed settled people" and hence the whole concept of rehabilitation and re-assimilation comes into play. I, however disagree with this theory for reasons that I will now outline.

Firstly, it is important to remember that in the United States there are more that 10,000 Irish Travellers with names like Collins, Sherlock, McDonagh, Maughan, Carroll and Murphy, and a large contingent of these Travellers are located in South Carolina, Georgia and Texas. These Travellers play a large part in the history of Irish Travellers. They are very traditional in their lifestyle and very clearly identify themselves as being Irish Travellers. They have progressed along very similar lines to the Traveller families who live in Ireland. These Travellers, like the tens of thousands of displaced Irish who travelled on the "coffin" ships to America, left Ireland during the mid 19th century. They maintained all of the lifestyle, customs and marriage patterns of the Travelling people when they reached America. We can assume from this that these patterns were well established among the families long before they left Ireland and can conclude that Travellers predate the famine.

Living on the roadside in poverty-stricken Ireland (mid-nineteenth century)

It is very difficult to locate the exact time in history when Travellers came into existence. In a way they have always existed but the disasters in history like the famine would have swelled the ranks of Travellers on the road. Around the time of the Poor Law Commission

(1834), statistics show that there were more than three million people on the roadside in Ireland. Within that three million Travellers were easily identified because, unlike the people living on the roadside who were one generation and would move back to the land once they got the chance, Travellers on the roadside were more than one generation, (they were great-grannies and grandchildren) and would not, if given the choice, decide to live on the land.

I am not trying to prove the exact origins of Travellers in Irish society, but to disprove any theories that suggest that we only came about as a result of some disaster in Irish history. The perception that we are drop-outs or misfits, because either ourselves or our ancestors couldn't cope, is wrong.

Travellers in the 16th century

When people, from where was known as "Little Egypt", came to this part of Europe they became known as "Egyptians", and from this word the term "gypsies" was derived. A law was passed in 1562 during the reign of Queen Elizabeth I stating that it was illegal to be an Egyptian or a Counterfeit Egyptian. In Ireland the penalty for this was deportation. The English law which was much stricter in its punishment, stated:

> Those in the company or fellowship of vagabonds, commonly called or calling themselves Egyptians, and also those counterfeiting, transforming or disguising themselves as such by their apparel, speech or other behaviour, shall do so under pain of death.

There was a note explaining what this law meant, what its reasoning was and who it applied to. It also referred to a group of people who had the attire, work practice, similar marriage pattern, lifestyle and family groups as Egyptians, but who were not Egyptian. This described the Travellers to a "T", and so it seems that there were Travellers in Britain and Ireland in 1562.

The word "Gypsy" is a collective name for many different extended groups including Shinti, Rom, Calderash. Gypsies never established themselves in any great numbers in Ireland because their lifestyle and especially their work habits were already to be found in larger numbers among Irish Travellers and Ireland is only a small country.

Some gypsies may have inter-married with Travelling people just as some of those who lost their farms in Famine times may have joined with the Travellers.

"Tinkers" in the 12th century

If we go further back to the 12th Century we get the word "tinker" (Tinceard = Tin craft) appearing many times in written documents and there clearly was a group of Travelling crafts people who played an important role in Irish society and in the Irish economy. Owen McNeil wrote a book called "Phases of Irish History" in which he said: *"Today's Travellers are direct descendants of industrial communities that lived in Ireland in Celtic and pre-Celtic times."* This is a beautiful theory that comes through our own language. Our language is known as "Shelta" or "Gammon" or "Cant". We ourselves call it "Cant" or "Minceirtoiree". The word "Minceir" means Traveller and "Toiree" means talk, so together it means "Traveller talk". Languages can be cousins to one another like Germanic or English Languages. Language is the last thing that we have left that gives us our antiquity. The closest cousin to our language is Old Irish, which was spoken here before the 13th century. Some of the words used at that time are still used by Travellers today when we speak in our language. The words which we use today for a priest and for God have shown up in old documents in pre-Christian Ireland.

Travellers in ancient Irish mythology

Our tradition was a very oral tradition so there is very little written evidence. Normally, history is about kings and queens but there are bits and pieces of evidence that show us that Travellers did not just come about in the last couple of centuries. We, as a community, have existed for a long time. Even when you read the more famous stories particularly the Tain Bo Cooley, you will come across these landless people who are not accepted by either Maeve's army or Cu Culainn's. Yet they would fight for any side. These people would always be the best hunters, their tents would be up first, others were frightened of them and didn't want them with them. There are also lots of stories in Irish mythology that mention the existence of people who had a diverse identity and culture from mainstream society.

Whether you accept everything I have said or not, you must at least agree that our origins go back a long way and may indeed be "lost in the mists of time".

Travellers in Irish society today – three sub-groupings

If you look at Travellers in Ireland today, you can see three sub-groups emerging. The first group and the largest, has a certain number of family names and certain traditions especially marriage patterns and lifestyle that are slightly different to the other groups. The Travellers who belong to this group have a long nomadic tradition and are very confident about their identity as Travelling People. The second group comes from the tradition of the fairground, carnival and entertainment people. These people are very much part of Traveller culture now. A third group among us would be known to have a lot of contacts and relationships with the settled community and would even have married into the settled community. Back in the 1930's marriage into this third grouping of Travellers was frowned on by the other two groups, but today that has changed. These distinctions would have been a lot clearer and more pronounced in the past. Now, however, there is assimilation between the three groups but still, small differences remain.

Ethnicity and culture

Michael McDonagh

What constitutes an ethnic group?

An ethnic group is a community of people who have a long shared history (which I have described in looking at the origins of the Traveller community) and who fulfil the follow characteristics:

• Biologically self-perpetuating

This means that the members of a group marry within their own community. This is especially true for Travellers who not only marry within their own community, but who generally marry within their own extended family group, which explains the high percentage of first cousin marriages within the Traveller community. "Marriage for Travellers is more a socio-political alliance than a personal whim, and has profound implications for group membership." (Ní Shúinéir 1996)

• Shares fundamental cultural values

Travellers as an ethnic group share certain core values, (which are looked at in greater detail later in this chapter and in the subsequent chapters), such as nomadism, self-employment, the centrality of family in Traveller life etc.

• Makes up a field of communication and interaction (i.e. socially separate)

Travellers, as an ethnic group, deal with settled people at a business level e.g. through scrap-collecting and carpet- selling etc., but Travellers do not, by and large, mix with settled people. Travellers also have their own way of speaking English that settled people find hard to understand but which is readily understood by other Travellers, regardless of what part of the country they are in. In addition to this Travellers also speak their own language called Gammon or Cant.

• Has a membership which defines itself and is defined by others

You cannot become a Traveller, you are born one, and Travellers know exactly who belongs and who does not belong to their community. Settled people also describe Travellers by using certain, generally overwhelmingly negative, terms and settled people often talk about Travellers "redeeming" themselves by becoming "housed Travellers" or "settled Travellers" (Ní Shúinéar 1996)

• Subject to oppression

You only have to look at the daily papers and to the media in general for numerous examples of attacks on Travellers and of the harassment of evictions etc. For Travellers, discrimination is a part of everyday life, when they are refused services which settled people take for granted e.g. entry into shops, pubs, launderettes, or use of hotels for wedding receptions etc.

Cultural values which Irish Travellers share with other ethnic groups

Travellers share many of the same cultural values and patterns as Travellers worldwide and as Gypsies. Some areas of commonality include the following,

◆ Nomadism

◆ The dominant position of the family and the extended family and respect for older members of the family

◆ Early and close kin marriage

◆ Work patterns

◆ Rituals surrounding death and marriage patterns

◆ Relationship with the dominant settled society

◆ Shared field of communication

◆ Subject to discrimination, - from the extermination of a quarter of a million Gypsies and Travellers by the Nazis, to the discrimination practised in our own country today against the Traveller community

Culture

What it means to be a Traveller

If you ask a "country person" (see Glossary), "what are you?" the answer will be, "I'm a farmer," or "a postman" or "a teacher". Country people identify with the work they do and the more specialised, the better. They insist on defining Travellers in this way too; we used to be tinsmiths, now we are scrap dealers. But none of this makes any sense from a Traveller's point of view. Ask a Traveller, "What are you?" and the answer will be "I'm a McDonagh", or "one of the Joyce's" or "Collins".

To be a Traveller is to be part of a Community. In some ways Travellers and settled people use the term "Traveller" to mean mobility, but it does not mean mobility. Although being mobile is part of being a Traveller, it is not what a Traveller is. Being a Traveller means being part of a community that has a shared history, shared culture and an understanding of what it is like to be a Traveller. It's having a family with a support mechanism there. It's a way of life.

Traveller Culture

When I say that I have my own culture and lifestyle what do I mean? If I were to ask you to explain your culture to me you would find it a very hard thing to do, and yet people are always asking Travellers to explain their culture. Trying to look at Traveller culture in isolation is not the most prosperous way of approaching this subject, as it's not the wisest idea to pigeon-hole Traveller culture. We need to look at the overall context and how all the different aspects of Traveller culture fit together. Culture is something alive, something adapting and changing all the time. If we try to look at Travellers in a romantic way, and see the painted wagons, the green fields etc., we are looking into the past and nobody wants to live in the past, people want to live in the future. Travellers are not being allowed to change in a natural way, the way they would have all along, because now more than ever it's a forced change which has a negative effect.

I don't think you can paint a picture and definitively say, "This is Traveller culture!" There are many aspects of Traveller culture which are very subtle, such as the particular way in which you rear your children that allows them to survive within a society which is oppressive. Marriage patterns are another aspect of culture where the majority of Travellers would only marry other Travellers in order to strengthen the identity or the bond of Travellers. Some aspects of Traveller culture include nomadism, independence and flexibility in economic adaptation, resistance to wage labour in favour of family-based self-employment, religious rituals etc.

My culture is everything about me, how I think, how I act, how I make decisions and everything else that is important to me. Travellers are an ethnic group. If we talk about Travellers having an ethnic identity it means that we have a common history, language, religion etc. Another characteristic that makes us members of an ethnic group is that you are born a Traveller, you cannot become one.

When working with people from an ethnic group it is helpful to make sure that you are trying to see value in their life rather than dismissing their lifestyle or putting them down. It is only in the last number of years that people started to work with Travellers and see them as people with an identity of their own, despite the fact that there was clear recognition on behalf of law–makers that Travellers existed as a separate group because historically a whole series of laws were passed against the very existence of Travellers or Gypsies in many European countries. (McCarthy 1996)

In a way Travellers were ashamed of their identity because for years we were told to give up our traditions and ways. As it is, many of our traditions are gone forever. When you take away a person's identity, as has happened to many Travellers, it causes unbelievable problems. This happened in the 1960's and generated very low self-esteem among Travellers. Many have a fierce inferiority complex which has only been tackled in the last few years. It's great to see the difference in young people now. They are proud to be Travellers and they want to keep their language, whereas a couple of years ago they were hiding the fact that they were Travellers. Many were trying "to fit in". If you went into a shop and other Travellers came in you would ignore them and not look them in the eye, because they were "letting the side down" by not dressing "to fit in". Could you imagine not being yourself or having to deny that your grandparents ever existed because they were Travellers and you no longer wanted to be a Traveller? We were expected to assimilate. What helps us not to assimilate are the two most important aspects of our culture as I see them, family and nomadism.

Family — the centre of Traveller culture

All that happens in the lives of Travellers, from birth to death, all the big family gatherings, the christenings, the marriages and funerals, are of huge importance because these are the events that mark different stages of our lives from beginning to end. Not only do these occasions play a role for the immediate family who are directly involved in the event but also for the extended family and that's why sometimes there would be huge gatherings of people coming together for an occasion.

It's important to remember that within Traveller society you have a mother, father and children, but that is not as important as the family group which would consist of the immediate family and the uncles, aunts, cousins, grandparents, second and third cousins. You have one extended family and this is not seen in geographical terms. Settled people organise themselves within parishes and districts. Travellers organise within families. My family has relations in Dublin, the Midlands, London and Galway. If you look at different names you can immediately identify them with a family group. Our family is McDonagh which is the most popular name among Irish Travellers, followed by Ward, Collins, Joyce, and Nevin. If you go south you have the O'Driscolls, O'Briens, Sullivans. Galway names are Sweeney and Ward and in Clare you have Sherlocks. Ward is a very popular name. The Irish version means "son of the Bard" and in the past the Travellers were the bards.

Extended family is really important. It is important that it is kept together. All the support mechanisms and everything that allows us to survive as Travellers are within it. Working at your family ties is the key to Traveller identity so we will turn up at all meetings of the extended family, for weddings, for funerals or when visiting the sick in hospital. If you even look at what happens in hospital when someone's sick or dying, everyone gathers together and visits the hospital, and the nurses are going haywire over the huge number of Travellers there. I think that it's very important to understand that for Travellers this is a sign of respect that shows the person who is going to die that their life was worthwhile and that their life just didn't go by unnoticed. In addition to this there is also the whole grieving process whereby we openly mourn for the person who has died. This explains the reason why for generations there has been a prejudice on our behalf where we see settled people go to a funeral and we say to ourselves, "God they mustn't have loved the people they're burying because they're not crying or expressing strong emotions very visibly and openly." It's important for Travellers to actually be allowed to express their grief because it's part of the grieving process.

Nomadism

Michael McDonagh

The nomadic mind-set

Nomadism is more than travelling from A to B. It is everything about Travellers. I live in a house and have done so for a long time but that doesn't make me a settled person. Many country people (see Glossary), who call themselves "settled", may in fact travel more than some Travellers, but this does not make them nomadic. Nomadism is your whole outlook on life. It's how you view life and it means that you see things in a different light, i.e. work, accommodation, education etc. The physical fact of moving is just one aspect of a nomadic mindset that shows in every aspect of our lives. Nomadism entails a way of looking at the world, a different way of seeing things, a different attitude to accommodation, to work and to life in general.

Nomadism affects all aspects of Traveller life, even death. The standard way of coming to terms with bereavement is to move away from memories of the dead person. Just as settled people remain settled people even when they travel, Travellers remain Travellers even when they are not travelling. Travellers who are not moving can, and do, retain the mindset of a nomad. This is why I feel it is important to speak of "nomadism" rather than "travelling" with regard to Travellers. As the E.C. synthesis report, (*Liégeois, Gypsies and Travellers 1987*) puts it,

> A Traveller is someone who remains detached from his surroundings, who is able to pick up and move whenever it is useful or necessary to do so, when he needs to or simply feels like it. There is an important difference between the objective reality of travelling (the fact of moving from one place to another) and the subjective reality: feeling oneself to be a Traveller. Nomadism is as much a state of mind as a state of fact.

The functions of nomadism

Travellers do not wander about aimlessly with no precise goal to meet. For Travellers nomadism fulfils many functions vital to their very survival. I will discuss these under three broad headings – social, economic, and cultural – while emphasising that there is no such division in real life.

Social

Travellers travel in small groups of closely related nuclear families, but we understand our family membership in terms of the vast extended family. When we travel we meet up with other family members often with a social occasion such as a wedding or funeral involving a family member as the focus of the get-together. Even families who are sedentary for most of the year feel a lot of joy and happiness when setting out on a journey although it may only be a short one. These feelings are very much in evidence in the way Travellers participate in the Annual Traveller Walking Pilgrimage.

Getting together with other members of the family also serves many practical functions, for example, finding suitable marriage partners. Some Traveller parents arrange their children's matches (preferably within the extended family). Marriages take place within the family. When I speak about marriage, I would lean more towards matched marriages, because in my opinion they work. Many settled people have difficulty with understanding that. It is important to remember that not all Traveller families believe as strongly as others in matched marriages. Different families have different traditions and it is never possible to generalise about Travellers.

Keeping in touch through travel also means keeping tabs on family members which applies to everyone. When people meet, they pass on news, including scandal. Travellers live their lives balanced on a thin line, their every move watched by the whole family. If they do anything that brings them to crossing this line they'll be let know about it in many ways by many people. And if they cross that line, it will be very, very hard to get back on the right side of it.

Keeping up with the news, building contacts, strengthening relationships, etc. are all strong reasons for travelling. Just as travelling gives an opportunity of meeting up with people, it also makes it possible to avoid people. This is of importance to Travellers. When arguments arise, being able to move on means keeping the conflict from becoming too serious.

The social reality of nomadism is however far greater than the mere fact of travelling. Country people organise every aspect of their lives (from neighbourhood watch to parishes to electoral constituencies) on the fact of sedentarism, the fact that they live permanently side-by-side with a fixed group of other people. Travellers, on the other hand, organise every aspect of their lives around family ties, how far away other family members may be is of no importance, anymore than how physically close non-family may be. Travellers need to keep in touch and this in turn requires travel.

Economic

Travel is essential to our economic survival. If you look at how Travellers work, the whole family unit would be an economic unit and in the past Travellers would move around in small working families. For the survival of a community it doesn't make sense to have a huge extended family moving together or living together and working together, because Travellers couldn't make a living that way. If you allow a large extended family grouping to move together it has disastrous effects on the whole working life of Travellers. Yet the whole policy in regard to accommodation pushes very much in that direction. Now Travellers are forced to travel further afield to actually survive.

Cultural

Nomadism is a fundamental part of Traveller identity. Many of our values such as the family network and the support systems it provides are directly related to it.

The Irish Traveller Movement, in need of a logo, ran a competition, and it was interesting to see the symbols chosen by the entrants. The recurring themes were horses, horseshoes, wheels, wagons, and tents, even from young Travellers born and reared in houses who had never been on the road.

The importance of nomadism expresses itself in material culture. Trailers and vans are important symbolically and financially.

> Travellers' material culture, the trailers and the vans, facilitate their nomadism and are symbolically important, a fact that is frequently misinterpreted by the settled world. Travellers spend their money on what they can take with them when travelling and therefore a significant percentage of their expenditure is on transport- cars and vans and specifically on the kind of transport that enables them to earn a living. Transport has a much higher priority and significance for Travellers, precisely because they are nomadic.
>
> (McCarthy 1996)

Another important symbol of nomadism is jewellery. Like other nomadic peoples all over the world, Irish Travellers carry their wealth by wearing it. I remember when I was told that I was going to get married, my first thought was "I'll have to buy her a gold cross and chain." Nobody told me to do it, I just knew that this was what you did and over the years, you'd collect other little bits and pieces. Then, when things are at their worst, you always have that to fall back on; it's only ever as a last resort, when you're short of food or money, you'd fall back on that piece of jewellery.

Travellers' attitude to property is coloured by nomadism. "They have little interest in material things for their own sake, only as readily realizable assets to be disposed of ready for a new start after a move". (Binchy 1996)

Nomadism and accommodation

Fear of being sedentary

Traveller's view of accommodation differs vastly from that of country people. Travellers see accommodation as a stopping place regardless of whether their stay turns out to be a long or a short one. Whether living on a halting site or in a house, any kind of accommodation is seen in a temporary capacity. Temporary could mean anything up to twenty or thirty years. In the past you had summer and winter camps. Houses are seen as winter camps. When you as a Traveller go into a house it is one of the most frightening experiences you can have. It is a realisation that this is where you could stay for the rest of your life. This is it! Some Travellers have become physically sick from being in houses and realising that the authorities are expecting them never to move out. It's hard to imagine what it is like for people to say, "This is the end of the road!"

I remember when I first got a house, my grandfather looked at me and said, "Michael, that's all very well for the winter but how will you feel when the spring comes in, and you'll see the bumblebee buzzing at your window?" I was eighteen or nineteen years old and at first it was lovely but when I was talking with my settled neighbours a week later they were talking about what they would be doing to these houses in thirty years time. To me that was a whole lifetime away. Travellers think from day to day. If things are going wrong today, sure maybe they'll be right tomorrow. If you haven't got it today, sure you'll have it next week. I was happy in that house but when women were going on about mortgages in thirty years time, that frightened me. I wondered what I was letting myself in for. We left nine or ten months later. Living in a group housing scheme with Travellers, I feel happier because I know tomorrow I can go back on the side of the road if I want to. If you put in central heating and other Travellers see you, they'd say you were there for life. So if they said that, I'd be gone next week. In some cases, Travellers have become depressed when they move into houses and never adjust to living in one place permanently. Many Travellers have left houses for this reason.

Most Travellers who live in houses are content enough, as long as they know and feel they can move on when they need to. When they have the option of travelling, they have peace of mind, even though they may not actually exercise that option. But if Travellers get into a situation where they feel that they are being forced to settle in a place, that they are being blocked from moving on, it's a different story. If that happened most Travellers would not have any peace of mind and in most cases they would move on. When I was the Accommodation Officer of the National Council for Travelling people, I talked to Travellers all over the country about their fears in regard to moving into a house. I wanted to understand these feelings and one way I had of finding out was by asking them, "How would you feel if you were told that you had to stay exactly where you are now, for the rest of your life?" The reaction was just horror.

The regressive concept of "re-settlement"

The Report of the Commission on Itinerancy 1963 pushed the concept of "re-settlement", which suggested that resettling Irish Travellers was the only way forward. Committees were set up around the country and the people involved were well-intentioned and positive. Although they were doing their best to help they were going about it the wrong way. People came from all over the world to work with us. We were even photographed for the National Geographic! The process was all wrong because it saw us as the problem. It didn't see us as people with accommodation problems. It certainly didn't see us as people with a distinct culture. Even the title wasn't right. The Commission gave us the name "itinerant" which most Travellers have no time for and don't really like. We would never call ourselves itinerants instead we call ourselves Travellers or Travelling people. (We don't like knackers or tinkers either. Travellers call each other tinker as a compliment they might say, "he's a very good tinker". The younger people use it as a derogatory term.)

Opposition to Traveller accommodation

When proposals for a new halting site or group housing scheme are mentioned, we very often see a group of residents protest against Travellers. Whenever there is a complaint (made by a residents' group or by an individual) in regard to accommodation for Travellers for whatever the reason, devaluation of property, etc., Travellers are prevented once more from getting better living conditions. It's unbelievable the number of babies that have died in this country because of the conditions they live in. People don't devalue property, attitudes do. When you use your own power to stop any person from getting better facilities and living conditions you are contributing to them dying. Nobody ever wants to see the end results of their actions but deep down we must realise when we have done something wrong. Getting water and toilet facilities for children may help them to live.

Poor design and location of units of accommodation

"The design prevents access to the back of the houses, leaving only enough space to be able to walk around to the rear. Design is substandard; in some cases they resemble the old 'tigeens'." This was my description, in 1983, of the new local authority housing for Travellers, when I was asked to look into this as part of my work as Accommodation Officer for the National Council. Some people may say that such bad design is carried out, out of ignorance of our lifestyle. Those in power are well aware of the needs of Travellers and design accommodation to prevent us from maintaining our culture, work patterns and our social ties.

Another aspect of accommodation, apart form the design, is location. Sites are to be found next to tip-heads and cemeteries and up the sides of mountains in the middle of nowhere. Nobody, Traveller or settled, would choose to live in such places, and many Travellers refuse to. More than one site has lain idle from the day it was opened because of this.

Traveller accommodation – the way forward

Local authorities have provided accommodation and made people fit into those structures. What needs to be done is to provide structures for people, not vice versa. Doing the opposite all along has done damage to Travellers. When services are being provided nobody consults with Travellers. If they did consult with us things would work out a lot better.

Accommodation is a temporary thing, so you have to understand that. It may be temporary in the long- term sense or it may not. To travel in Ireland today is becoming more and more difficult, if not impossible. One has only to look at the roadsides to see huge boulders blocking the places where Travellers could have stopped. Mounds of clay and rubble and deep trenches all serve the same purpose. The blocking up of traditional halting places all around the country has been a systematic move to leave Travellers with no place to go. In future, when we look at these boulders, will we see them as a monument to prejudice? One of the effects of the present accommodation policy is that when Travellers move into an area, they are afraid to move out, because the camp will be blocked up and they will be unable to return. So, for many Travellers, the only time they feel free to travel is when they have acquired a more permanent place to come back to. The policy of forcing Travellers to stay put in large, mixed groups, has eaten into our social structure, economic base and cultural identity.

The education system – catering for a nomadic people

Educating for life

One of the basic tools of life is education and I think it is very important for Travellers to get an adequate education. There are a huge number of Travellers who would be classed as being highly educated in terms of their ability to read, to communicate or to write, but who are unable to avail of their skills because their whole self- esteem has been taken away in the process of giving them that education. I think it is of huge importance that when Travellers are being educated that they are educated in a way that not only ensures that they receive the basics in education but also ensures that they receive an education for life which allows their identity to be developed, celebrated and resourced.

It's not good enough and it is a huge worry among Travellers that if they send their children to school that they might come out the other side not actually knowing who they are. This has happened to many people. The fact that there hasn't been a huge number of Travellers who have gone through the education system and come out the other side with their identity maintained discourages Travellers from sending their children to school. We need not only to provide an education for Travellers, but also to give them role models and to have positive discrimination to allow Travellers to get through the education system to the other side, all the while maintaining their identity.

Adapting to the limitations on nomadism in Ireland today

If you look all around, a number of families practice travelling a lot and in some cases you can see how they have shunned society because they wanted their own children to lead their lives in a particular way. A lot of these families have had very prosperous lives in more ways than others. As far as their identity is concerned, they're very proud of surviving extremely well economically. They own very nice houses, although that doesn't necessarily mean they live in these houses all the time. On the other hand, you see families who have been assimilated and have become more sedentary. Then, there are very sad cases where you would see the family break up. You would see the deprivation and the very negative aspects of settled society which they would have adopted and taken on.

The current situation in Ireland is one in which a range of powerful forces work together to limit nomadism. Many Travellers have successfully adapted to these limitations. They survive economically, socially and culturally, with a strong and positive sense of their Traveller identity. The most outstanding success story of how some Travellers respond to the limitations put on nomadism is that of the Rathkeale Travellers. These families are highly nomadic for much of the year, travelling throughout the British Isles and lately also the United States. The fact that they are doing very well economically is clear to anybody; but what is surprising about them is their better-than-average knowledge of Gammon. On second thought, however, this is not surprising: Gammon is a living language for them, because they are so active in trading. These Travellers upset the apple cart for settled policy-makers (who fail to recognise how the Travelling way of life can fit in with the modern world) by being "living contradictions" to their policy and who, because of this are not recognised as being Travellers at all. Council officials define them as "traders" not Travellers. When I talked with the Rathkeale Travellers, and told them that as far as policy-makers are concerned, they are "traders", not Travellers, they said, "Well Michael, you've met us, and you've talked with us and we would ask you now, that any time you hear that kind of talk, to stand up and tell the truth: that we are Travellers and proud to be Travellers". To this day, many Travellers that are the most nomadic are also the most economically successful and also have far less difficulty with their identity than people forced into settlement. And yet settled people are not able to see this; for them, just being mobile is negative and wrong in itself. Most families cope with the limitations put on them in a whole range of different ways.

However, at the other end of the scale are those who have been unable to cope. The policy of forcing Travellers to stay put in large mixed groups, has eaten into Travellers' social structure, economic base and cultural identity. We have already seen how all of these strands of culture are bound up with nomadism – they cannot function without it. For example, as members of the extended family lose touch, parents have a smaller number of suitable potential marriage partners for their children. Family support systems break down. People step out of line with no one to put them back on the right track. To quote a Council of Europe document, (*Liégeois Gypsies and Travellers 1987*), "When travel becomes just a dream, a long-delayed dream for the Traveller, despair and its effects set in (illness, breakup of the family, aggressiveness and delinquency). The result is a crisis in the society."

It's not simply about having nomadism taken away. The policy-makers who do this also ensure that Travellers are getting a great deal of "help" to "integrate" into "the community". The system makes people dependent on it, taking pride and independence away with one hand and giving the dole and second-hand clothes with the other. It makes no secret of its mission to "help the poor unfortunates", to "rehabilitate" Travellers; and Travellers, seeing how they are regarded, may internalise this low, negative self-image. Once they have accepted that being a Traveller is something to be ashamed of, the next step is to try to change, to become a settled person. And once you do that, you're lost, because settled people won't accept you, and Travellers won't want you any more than you want them to. Where does that leave you? Without your identity. Many Travellers find themselves stuck in limbo, with parents ashamed of their relatives and children ashamed of their parents.

Government policy on nomadism

Anti – nomadic policy

It would be untrue to say that nomadism is never mentioned in government policy. It is mentioned many times – in fact, it is seen as the entire "problem" to be "solved". Prohibition Orders came under the *"A Local Government Sanitary Services Act 1948"*. According to this Act, once accommodation exists, prohibition orders barring all Travellers from every other part of the area come into effect. Thus prohibition orders criminalise Travellers for the very fact of being Travellers. The Constitution gives central importance to the family within Irish society. The effect of prohibition, both in the past and today, very often is the break up of families.

From 1963 onwards there have been many groups, committees and other bodies that have influenced and helped shape government policy in regard to nomadism or rather, "itinerancy" as it was re-named. The *Report of the Commission on Itinerancy 1963*, which influenced other subsequent government policies stated the following,

> All efforts directed at improving the lot of itinerants and at dealing with the problems created by them, and all schemes drawn up for these purposes, must always have as their aim the eventual absorption of the itinerants into the general community.

This Report was the start of a long drawn-out campaign to get rid of nomadism suggesting that all schemes should take them away from their nomadic way of life and absorb them into the general community ("rehabilitation") and blaming Travellers as creators of the problem.

The Commission went on to say that, "insofar as the itinerants are concerned, absorption into the general community can be achieved only by a policy of inducing them to leave the road and settle down." The methods used to induce Travellers were, and are, severe:

> It should be made an offence with adequate penalties, (including imprisonment), for itinerants to camp within a stipulated radius of an approved camping site provided by a local authority (and later that,) any special difficulties and obstacles in the way of itinerant families obtaining any of the State or local authority allowances for which they are eligible should be eliminated as far as possible as a means of inducing them to settle.

Following the publication of the Report such voluntary bodies, known as Itinerant Settlement Committees, were set up all over the country. The aim of many of these Committees was, and in some cases still is, to "settle" Travellers and get them assimilated into the settled community.

It was not until twenty years after the original Report that a second official government policy statement, this time from *The Travelling People Review Body 1983*, was issued. Many of the recommendations and statements in this report seem at first to be very progressive and forward thinking; this unfortunately is not at all true. Consider, for example, the following statement, listed as a basic objective:

> To provide within a relatively short number of years a house for all Traveller families who desire to be housed. Travellers who are not so accommodated cannot hope to receive an adequate education. Nor can they avail satisfactorily of services such as health and welfare which are of such significance in the life of all people.

Here we see a recommendation that families who desire a house should be provided with one but, if they don't want a house, they cannot avail satisfactorily of services; no provision is made for meeting the educational needs of nomadic families.

On the face of it, there is a very big difference between "solving the itinerant problem" and recognising that "the decision to remain mobile is theirs and must be respected." This change can be illustrated very dramatically with two quotations from Charles J. Haughey. As Parliamentary Secretary to the Minister for Justice, he addressed the inaugural meeting of the Commission on Itinerancy in July 1960: *"there can be no final solution of the problems created by itinerants until they are absorbed into the general community" (The Report of the Commission on Itinerancy, 1963).*

Thirty-one years later, addressing the Fianna Fail Ard-Fheis as Taoiseach, he had a very different message:

> Local Authorities throughout the country will be called upon to take a special urgent action in this anniversary year to meet the needs of all Travellers within their area and we should respect the culture of our Travelling community and develop a better public understanding of their time honoured way of life. (Presidential Address, 1991).

The rhetoric has certainly changed but has the practice?

The future of Traveller accommodation

Now is a time of transition and of uncertainty, but I feel that this is a very hopeful sign. There are new moves towards policies based on partnership with Travellers, and on recognition of Travellers' ethnicity. Here at home, there is the Irish Traveller Movement, a national movement of both Travellers and settled people who support our claims. Irish people generally are more outward looking now, with more contact with, and more openness to, new ideas. As settled people get more used to listening to ideas from Italy and Belgium, they may be more willing to listen to ideas from the Irish Traveller Movement which has links with Gypsy and Traveller organisations all over Europe, and there is Irish Traveller representation on the world Romani Congress

At the end of the day, the problems faced by Travellers today can be traced back to the interference of settled people who, with their "settlement" committees, have done all they could to solve the "itinerant" problem by putting a stop to itinerancy, to nomadism. From 1963 onwards, settled people were certain what they wanted to do, and how to go about doing it. At present, however they are no longer so sure. There are two reasons for this firstly the old ideas haven't worked; second, Travellers themselves are standing up and saying so.

The Traveller economy

Michael McDonagh

"Travellers are economic nomads, providing marginal services to a generally hostile wider community" (Kenrick 1996).

1950's and 60's Ireland – a period of great change for Irish Travellers

The greatest period of change for Travellers in Irish society was from the 1950's and 1960's onwards. Prior to that we were mostly a rural people who were stuck in a boreen somewhere and not seen. Older people would say they'd never seen a town until they were thirteen or fourteen years of age. In rural Ireland Travellers would have been involved in providing services working as tin-smiths, seasonal farm labourers, door to door sales people, flower sellers. When Travellers moved near towns and cities in the 1960's they became a very visible group. The outskirts of towns and cities became very attractive for Travellers, so they had to adapt and develop new skills to respond to the emerging needs. When social welfare came about Travellers couldn't avail of it because they had to have a permanent address.

Travellers are now involved in a broad range of activities; for example, buy and sell market trading, scrap collecting, tarmac laying and antique dealing. Some Travellers have now entered the mainstream labour force and others are involved in providing a service to their own community i.e. as youth and community workers, childcare assistants and in health promotion work. While the range of work has changed the manner in which these activities are organised has remained constant.

Travellers' perception of work

Travellers are more concerned with generating income as opposed to creating jobs. The Traveller economy is also based on providing services on an immediate cash basis. Travellers will try their hand at almost anything if there's a reward in it or something to be achieved in return. Travellers, however, don't see work in the same light as settled people would. For Travellers, work is not something that you do from an early age to a retirement age. The prospect of this would frighten them. The whole idea of routine and being very structured or strict on time-keeping is something that many Travellers haven't got their heads around. Nevertheless, Travellers are adapting and changing and some are very comfortable being in a routine and taking on a job that may last five or six years. Although Travellers are still very much in the frame of mind that courses or jobs which are immediate, short, snappy and enjoyable are great, there is a change and they are now asking themselves whether they can get a real job out of the course and they are also feeling that being on the dole isn't as good an option as it was in the past. In addition to this, there is greater pressure on Travellers today (and indeed on people in general), to be more materialistic. In the past people were satisfied with less, but now they are obsessed with having the latest clothes, whether it's Nike or Adidas, and this means that more and more money is needed and so people are beginning to realise that if there are jobs out there that will pay you enough, then it makes sense to get a job.

Economy and nomadism

Nomadism is also a key feature of the Traveller economy. Travelling is part of attending markets and fairs and of doing seasonal work such as potato or fruit picking. Travellers must travel to earn their living, be it by scrap collection, hawking or recycling waste. Travel is essential to our economic survival. Travellers spot a gap in the market and respond to it. Because they can move from one area to another very quickly this enables them to make a profit in areas others have found to be non-productive in economic terms. Some of the most successful and richest Traveller families are those who have adapted to the present conditions best and are very mobile between Ireland, England and the Continent. Due to their nomadic lifestyle and way of thinking, plans are not long-term and if you said to a Traveller that they would still be in their present job in ten years time they would be frightened to death. Short-term work and seasonal work suited Travellers in the past and they still think this way to an extent as when you hear young boys saying that "Christmas is coming" and they need a job for a couple of months.

A self-employed family-based economy

The family is the basic economic unit of the Traveller economy and self-employment is the essential characteristic of this family-based economy. Being your own boss is the important thing, being free to fit your work into the demands of the extended family. Travellers in self employment can more easily respond to the social and cultural demands required of them by their own community, than is possible in a permanent job. Travellers dislike "manager-worker" type relationships, especially if the employer is a settled person because, as Pavee Point states, Travellers want to ensure that "they are free to pursue their own cultural priorities without conflict", (*Recycling and the Traveller Economy 1993*). For example, it is important for Travellers to be free to attend funerals, or other family occasions that may take place in other parts of the country. All members of the family, young and old, have a role to play in generating an income. Children help their mothers by minding younger children, shopping, cleaning and young Traveller boys prepare for their apprenticeship through developing an eye for the scrap they collect at an early age. An apprenticeship scheme is also in operation in the Traveller community where skills are passed on from one generation to the next within the family structure. What you actually work at is of very little importance, you look for opportunities and make the best of them.

Home space and work space tend to be one and the same within the Traveller economy. This is a characteristic of the nomadic lifestyle. It also means that it is very important for local authorities to keep this in mind when planning a group housing scheme or a halting site. There needs to be space for work. But today so many of the local authorities make it a condition of living on a site that you don't collect scrap etc. Yet, *The Report of Task Force on the Travelling Community 1995* recommends that "The design and construction of Traveller specific accommodation should include limited storage /workspace. Such space is seen as the first step in the development of trading activity under planned conditions".

Flexibility

Flexibility is another characteristic of the Traveller economy. Travellers won't rely on one way to make a living. There is always change happening. When one way of earning a living is gone another will take its place. Travellers adapt to survive and respond to what is needed in mainstream society at any given time. Recycling started around towns when Travellers started to work with the enormous amount of waste that settled people were throwing away. Travellers were into recycling before it was fashionable and we're proud of that. I remember Pavee Point doing a study (*Recycling and the Traveller Economy 1993*) and they found that approximately 50% of scrap metal collected and supplied to scrap merchants is collected by the Traveller community, that approximately 400 jobs in the settled community are generated by Traveller recycling initiatives and that approximately

£6 million is generated in the Irish economy through Travellers working with scrap.

Travellers and the social economy

In my opinion, Travellers fit very well into the area of the social economy that is being talked so much about nowadays. *The Report of the Task Force on the Travelling Community 1995* mentions this idea of a "social economy" and quotes a European Union report which states that, "the social economy exists within the continuum of possibilities ranging from supply totally protected by public subsidies to totally competitive supply" (*Growth, Competitiveness, Employment, 1993*).

The social economy covers local services, environmental protection, recycling waste and general improvements in the quality of life, especially in disadvantaged communities. The Task Force also goes on to say, (quoting the EU white paper), that there is a need for,

> a widening of the concept of work, incorporating all forms of paid or partially paid work within a common framework comprising the social economy, intermediate employment enterprises and the informal economy.
> (*The Report of the Task Force on the Travelling Community 1995*)

Travellers entire economy is informal but it is true to say that most settled people view it negatively. I think this is because many settled people see Travellers as second-class citizens because the perception is that they are involved with the "black" or " informal" economy, which they see as illegal. This raises questions about how the members of Irish society view work which the European Union White Paper suggests is an area which needs to be looked at.

Travellers are also seen by many settled people as being dependent on hand-outs and "the dole". The fact, is however, that many Travellers are engaged in a wide range of economic activities. Due to the fact that they value self-employment and are very flexible and mobile, Travellers are in fact less dependent and passive than settled people's perceptions would make them out to be. The qualities of enterprise and initiative that are present in the Traveller community are now coming to be valued and recognised as the development of the social economy is seen as a way forward for the Irish and European economy.

The Report of the Task Force on the Travelling Community 1995 commissioned research into economic and employment development policies in Australia that target indigenous Australian groups such as the Aborigines. The research showed that there was a need for specific identifiable posts within the public sector which require an intimate knowledge of the indigenous group and their culture and an ability to communicate effectively with them. This research could be usefully re-designed and applied within the Irish context in reference to Travellers. These positions would be in the area of service provision for Travellers and, with these criteria, should become more open for Travellers. I have always found it very difficult to understand how services for people such as Travellers are normally provided by settled people. This would be one area for Travellers to be involved in, in the social economy whereby Travellers could be trained to become service-providers for their own community, so that services for Travellers would be provided by Travellers. This would be a more progressive way of actually delivering a quality service.

It is quite clear that the Traveller economy has a role to play in the larger area of the social economy. It is also evident that a number of Travellers are now taking on different types of work and you might even go to places where you'll find Travellers driving taxis, working in supermarkets, etc. and I regard this as important progress. Regardless of whatever type of work Travellers become involved in, in the future, if Travellers have to hide their identity to get a job or to earn a living then the results will be disastrous.

The way forward – responding to the challenge to embrace difference

When we talk about the Travelling community it's not just a question of whether they would prefer serviced halting sites. It's that they want their culture recognised, they want to be full citizens of this country. I think that the most important things are that there's real space for their own self-development and self-expression, that we have space for them and that we value them; and that the other things like the appropriate kind of houses, services and facilities are provided to the best of our ability as a nation. But perhaps the most important thing is that we value them as a distinct community within our larger community.

(Extract from a speech given by President Robinson at Pavee Point 1990)

President Robinson's words express the new spirit of pluralism and the power of imagination to move out of narrow-minded thinking and to move forward in a more accepting manner, with an understanding that differences can be complementary rather than a source of division.

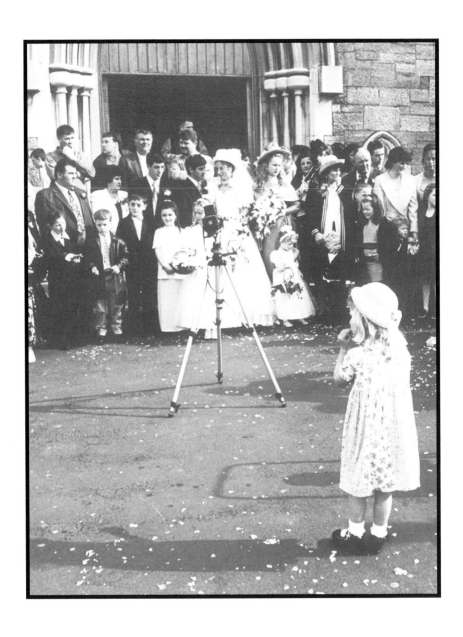

Family, Marriage and Faith: changing times in the Traveller community

Winnie McDonagh

When you're talking about family to Travellers, especially those who like me have a large extended family, it can sometimes be a blessing and a curse! I grew up with a big immediate and extended family and have been surrounded by family all my life. Having a family around you is a blessing but sometimes you can need to have a bit of space to yourself to get away even from the immediate family. Because I work and the type of work which I do involves meeting and working with people all day, I like to be on my own when I get a bit of spare time. You might be sitting in the trailer and you might want to read a book or look at your own television programme, or just be quiet, and people will be coming in and out for a visit or a chat. You would say to yourself, "if I could just get rid of them or be on my own for a half hour!" That's when you realise the downside.

The past

There is however good support in families, they do try to help out and can be great in a crisis or difficulty. This seems to be changing however and there is a sense that when we recall the past there seems to have been more support among the families back then. I can remember when I was growing up that there were particular roles that certain people in the family and extended family played which were very direct and very clear. There wouldn't have been a problem in the past with an uncle or an aunt having a more direct say in a particular situation or giving some kind of advice or support. In a way it was almost as if the extended family was part of your immediate family as well, so aunts and uncles and grannies played a big part and filled these roles. In the past there was more of a collective decision or discussion about what went on.

The present

What I see happening today is similar to what is happening in the settled community, whereby families themselves are withdrawing more into themselves and are becoming more distant from the extended family. People don't feel that they should or can impose their views or their beliefs on other members of the family. There appears to be an uncertainty or discomfort about this. We have young people today who feel they must stand on their own two feet and do their own thing. They feel that they must be able to support themselves and their own immediate family and sort out their own problems and they feel that they shouldn't be going to either Mammy, Daddy or anyone else to solve their problems. There is a good and bad side to that way of thinking. Sometimes, the fact is that the young people are not strong enough or experienced in themselves for all that they have to cope with today and they miss out on having the support and help of the family. At the same time you have to get the balance right because, if you have too many people giving you their advice this can be even more confusing!

A time of transition

There has also been a change in the understanding of what family life means and nowadays a hundred and one different things are influencing people. Television is a huge influence and there is a feeling among older people (and I find myself agreeing with them) that younger people don't have the same respect for older people that they did in the past. The younger people are less likely to take advice from older people and yet the older people are very concerned about the direction in which the young people are going. Some of the older people are especially concerned and fearful about the increase in drug-taking and drinking in the community. In the past young people were not allowed to drink or were encouraged not to drink until they were in their twenties or later. Now what is happening is that the young people themselves are socialising more and are drinking at a much earlier age. To the older people they're only building up problems for themselves and their children in the future.

It seems that there has been a breakdown in communication and respect between families and the extended family that has been gradually taking place, and the role that older people played in the past is dying out now without anything positive to replace it. In the past you would have had certain people in the community who would be acting the role of counsellors or mediators, who would advise younger couples. This was something good and positive that has been lost. The result is that there are certain issues which are not being addressed or looked at. The type of support that was there in the past, is not there any longer, and in that sense the role of the extended family in the Traveller community is different and changing and there's nothing to replace it. So in regard to family support it is always good to have a family around you who can comfort you if you're going through a crisis or have a problem, but this is one of the areas in the Traveller community that I would see undergoing a lot of change in the near future, and sometimes it's not always for the best.

Marriage – different generations, different perspectives

In regard to marriage there have been many changes over the last number of years. The young people themselves have changed and the older generation in a sense is dying out. At the time when I was getting married, there was an older generation of grand-uncles, grand-aunts, grannies and great grandparents around who had a big influence on the younger people but sadly, they have now passed on. This older generation has completely died out and the elderly people that are here now are of a different generation and have themselves experienced different things. The younger people too have had different experiences and see things very differently.

For instance, the number of women of my mother's age who worked before or after marriage is, I'd say, very few. Most of these women were in the home looking after the children or trying to make a living from begging (i.e. door – to – door selling of goods in baskets). When I was a teenager, if you asked each woman, out of a group of twenty, to put up her hand if she was going out begging, I'd say nineteen, if not all of them, would. That has changed dramatically and if I did the same thing with a similar group today they would look at me as if to say, "What is she talking about? I would not go out begging!" Most of them now are on training courses of some kind or other.

One issue that has had a major impact on marriage in the Traveller community has been the growing number of separation and marital problems. This has become a serious concern for both middle-aged and older people. In a sense it has led to a questioning of the marriage patterns, traditions or customs ; for instance the short engagements, low marriage age, matched weddings etc. Some of the more traditional families are trying to hold on to those traditions and customs and are feeling very confused about whether they are something we need or should let go of. It raises a whole range of questions and concerns regarding the best thing to do for young people and about the sort of marriage patterns and traditions that were there. It is very difficult to decide what we need to let go of or what we should hold on to.

Forming relationships – "dating"

It is very important to remember that when talking about young people within the Travelling community, they have different patterns of dating or forming relationships to those of the settled community.

Whether or not I personally agree with how marriages take place within the Traveller community, I would still be very concerned if tomorrow morning the Travelling community of Finglas or elsewhere said "That's it, from tomorrow all our young people are going to be allowed to go out and date and form relationships in the same way as it is done in the settled community". I would also be concerned for the welfare of young Travellers going out to discos, youth clubs, pubs etc., because they haven't been brought up to deal with socialising or forming relationships in the same way as the settled community.

Whether it's a good or bad thing, the fact is that there is a different understanding of how a relationship is formed and develops within the Traveller community.

Arranged marriages – the advantages and disadvantages

Many settled people have difficulty understanding arranged marriages and there are a lot of misunderstandings in regard to arranged marriages. Some people think that an arranged marriage is something that you can do by just sitting down and saying to a person, "You'll marry him/her, and that's it." There is a lot more to it than that. The parents especially, will have some lengthy discussions before they consider a marriage. Arranging marriages is not as strict as what it was in the past. The young people have more opportunity to talk to each other, to find out each other's likes and dislikes and to see if they're suited.

At the present time, there is change here too ; the young Travellers' views on marriage are changing and they want to do things somewhat differently from what their parents would have done. That is not to say that certain individuals and families disagree with this and would wish to keep things as they were. In my opinion, many of the Travellers getting married nowadays would know more about their potential partner's family and background than many settled people do, even though they have been dating a person for a number of years. Young Traveller couples would know the history of their partner's family, their background etc.

In an arranged marriage what normally happens is that, within the family you will have a matchmaker or somebody, who could be an aunt or cousin etc. who will be asked to suggest a suitable match. Sometimes this person is on the lookout for two young people who would suit each other. If a young couple is seen to be compatible, the matchmaker will talk to the parents of the boy and discuss the possibilities and then with the girl's parents. If both sets of parents are happy, the boy is asked. If the boy is happy then the girl is asked. You won't usually hear about a match until all arrangements have been decided. The arranging of a marriage is an important business and is not to be taken on lightly. Not all Traveller families believe in arranged marriages as strongly as others do. Different families have different traditions or customs, which they may or may not follow and it is never wise to generalise about Travellers.

My own marriage and those of my brothers and sisters were arranged, so I am not totally opposed to this practice. Most young people like to think they have made their own choice and they often meet or see each other in this sense for the first time at social occasions such as weddings, engagement parties or at Christmas. But their families will have a say in who their son or daughter is marrying. Sometimes an older person will offer their advice even if it is to point out that, in their opinion, the couple are not suited, and this can be very valuable because choosing a partner for life is not an easy thing to do.

Marriage in the future

I am very aware however, due to the many changes in regard to marriage, such as the increase in separations and marital breakdown, that people are more cautious and are not as quick to match-make today as they were in the past. When arranging marriages, you're dealing with people's lives and it doesn't necessarily follow that a boy or girl coming from a good or stable family, will be the same themselves. I would be very reluctant to be a matchmaker myself and would be much happier to leave it to the two individuals themselves in the hope that they would be sensible and mature enough to know what they are doing. I realise that this is difficult for all concerned because of the restrictions that are on the young Traveller people from within the community, but I would hope that in time we would become more relaxed about this, without the young people having to lose respect for themselves or for their families.

In the past young people had very little, if indeed any, say in their choice of partner. Families didn't question themselves, at least not openly, about arranging marriages. Nowadays, Travellers are concerned about the future of their young people, about what's best for them in today's world, and there is a growing sense that things are changing and that what may have been considered good and suitable in the past is perhaps not so good today.

In the future I can see more mixing with settled people and perhaps more marriages taking place between Travellers and settled people. I also believe that matched marriages will still be there in some form, along with some of the other customs and traditions. I think that in fifty years time Travellers will still describe themselves as Travellers and will still feel that their customs, traditions, values and way of life are important to them. I don't think Travellers will ever become extinct or will allow themselves to become extinct. They will adapt and change and try to take the best of what's out there for themselves and for their families.

Faith

Traveller faith in the past

Another area, which has come into question for the Traveller community in recent years is the area of faith. In the past, faith was something that was fairly straightforward and something to be taken seriously. There were certain things that were done as a matter of course, for example confession, Sunday mass and the sacraments were obligatory and Travellers always said night prayers and followed other religious practices. I can still recall some of the prayers that I learned as a child and which you don't hear at all today.

The present – moving away from the institution

In recent years the Church itself has experienced a number of crises. There have been scandals and a lot of negative publicity in regard to the Church and this has had a significant impact on the Traveller community and its attitude to faith. As a result of these events many Travellers have lost faith in priests, nuns and the Catholic religion. To Travellers, the religious and clergy themselves seem to have lost faith in the Church. There has been a large fall in the numbers of young Travellers attending mass and many young people are questioning their individual faith.

The future – hunger for spirituality

I still believe, despite all that has happened recently regarding the church, that there is a very strong belief in God and His Blessed Mother among Travellers. Even though many young Travellers have distanced themselves from the organised Church, they still believe in prayer, Our Blessed Lady, the mercy of God, the saints. They may have lost their faith in the Church and priests, but they haven't lost their faith in God.

I think spirituality has become something personalised. There is no longer the need to put priests on pedestals. In the past, Travellers had huge respect for, and confidence in, priests and religious people but now they are coming to see priests as ordinary human beings who are not perfect but who can make mistakes and who don't have all the answers.

In the past the Church was seen as, and presented an image of itself as, having all the answers and having huge power and influence over people and all you had to do was believe in it and you would achieve salvation and everything would be alright. It still has power but the recent happenings have had a very big effect on how people now see those who are responsible for the Church here in Ireland, especially priests and bishops. This image or perception has been challenged and maybe this is for the better.

My faith

Personally, in regard to faith, I have my own personal opinions on religious issues. I can see the laity becoming much more involved in the life of the Church and, as is quite evident, there is a huge drop in the number of vocations. In the past the images that surrounded the Church were all very distant and removed from ordinary people, there was very little involvement of the people and even now it remains very selective. The people who have power and control of the Church now need to take a long hard look at how it can link back into people's lives in a very real way once again. I feel this is especially important for Travellers as they have always had a great belief in the Church, her priests and religious, and have felt very hurt and betrayed by what they have witnessed in recent times.

Traditional Music and the "master" performers from the Traveller community

Liam Gaul

The piper through the meadow straying

Masters of the Uileann Pipes

"A piper in the street to-day, set up and tuned and started to play, and away, away, away on the tide of his music we started". With those words of Seamus O'Sullivan I would like to introduce the reader to the wonderful world of traditional Irish music and the "Master" performers who came from the Irish Travelling People.

Today the Uileann pipes have survived and I am delighted to report are flourishing not alone in Ireland but in England, the United States of America and Australia with many fine performers of note. Names such as Davey Spillane, Paddy Moloney, Padraig MacMathuna, Peter Brown, Robbie Hannon and of course Liam O'Flynn have taken this folk instrument to the musical zenith, playing specially commissioned and composed works for Uileann pipes and orchestra. The credit for the survival of this much maligned folk instrument has to rest with the 'Master' performers and exponents from the Traveller Community in Ireland.

"Cash the Piper"- The pride of Wexford

The county of Wexford has a wealth of pipe music over the years with John Cash, born in 1832, being the leading exponent for over fifty years up to his death in December of 1906 at the age of 74 years. "Cash the Piper" was known the length and breadth of Ireland not just for his wonderful music but also for his combination of music with his trade of tinsmith and horse dealer and the results of such enterprises made Cash a comparatively wealthy man. A man of fine personal appearance, John Cash was always a most welcome figure at fairs, in particular at Scarawalsh which was always held on August 16th and the great fair of Enniscorthy where at the end of a day's horse dealing Cash would don the pipes for an evening's music. A popular song of the time features Cash as the leading figure and I quote:

"My name is "Cash the Piper"
And I'm seen at race and fair;
I'm known to all the jolly souls
from Wicklow to Kildare;
I've played at dance and wedding
from Bray to Clonegal,
But the cream of entertainment
Was with "Mick the Dalty's" ball

"Young Cash"- a Piper by trade

James Cash or "Young Cash" as he was known was a very famous piper born in October 1853 at the village of Kilmore, Co. Wexford. Unlike his father, James did not follow the 'trade' or deal in horses but made the playing of the Uileann pipes his career and the means of earning a living. This trait of professional piper became obvious at a very early age because when the Cash family lived in Wexford town young James went missing only to be found late in the evening surrounded on Main Street by a very appreciative crowd listening with rapt attention to the young lad's magical playing. Playing on his miniature set of pipes James had played a circuit of the town and was laden with more silver and copper coins than his youthful form could carry. As he grew to maturity James Cash's talents were sought by the top impresarios of the day as he fulfilled engagements at the leading theatres and music halls. He was a frequent visitor to Samuel Rowsome of Ballintore near Ferns where he was always accorded a warm welcome and the family's hospitality. After several years as a travelling piper James Cash died at Rathdrum in Co. Wicklow in 1980 bringing to an end a short and illustrious career.

"Johnny Doran", - the greatest piper in Ireland

"Johnny Doran, a famous piper" are the words inscribed on a headstone in Trinity Cemetery in Rathnew, County Wicklow. A simple statement but to anyone interested in the Uileann pipes this is the final resting place of the greatest piper Ireland ever produced and he came from the Travelling People. A well-dressed man of slight build, handsome, dark haired, with a ready smile showing firm white teeth and a soft spoken voice. That was Johnny Doran;

Johnny was born in 1908, one of a family of five daughters and four sons to John and Kathleen Doran of Rathnew, County Wicklow. It's easy to see why the piping tradition came down from this source as John Doran was a very fine piper himself. Eventually he taught his two sons Johnny and Felix to play, thereby ensuring this great tradition would carry on. As John Doran said, on being complimented on his fine piping by Donal Glennon as he played in a Dublin street, – "you should hear my two sons, Johnny and Felix play".

Those words became a reality for many interested musicians and listeners alike, for young Johnny Doran played at practically every fair and race meeting the length and breadth of Ireland. His brother followed in his footsteps some years later. Everyone who heard Johnny play was immediately entranced by his style of fast flowing ornamented piping - you almost had to dance. The Galway step dancer, Paddy Philbin remembers hearing Johnny for the first time as he played outside his caravan on a fine evening – he was so taken aback by the piping that he hadn't a step. On becoming friends with Johnny he often danced to his music outside the Imperial Hotel in Galway where Johnny always played on a Saturday evening when in that area.

Local musicians in places Johnny visited became firm and fast friends with him as he tripped out their favourite tunes – "Rakish Paddy", "The Steam Packet", "Tarbolton", "Colonel Frazer" and his favourite reel, "The Swallow's Tail". Martin Talty, Martin Rochford and of course the great Willie Clancy from Milltown Malbay played a lot of music with Johnny following him on his travels through their native county of Clare. It was Doran who introduced Willie Clancy to the Uileann Pipes and look what happened! Willie became famous throughout the world of piping. Johnny was an excellent music reader learning a lot of his repertoire from Capt. Francis O'Neill's collected works. Martin Talty recollects giving Johnny a 'new' tune in a manuscript form and after a few sightings of it on the Tin Whistle, Johnny would then transfer it to the pipes making his own of it with his individual ornamentation and style.

Johnny Doran played in the open air always standing using the pipes box to rest his foot upon giving him the elevation required to rest the regulators and drones across his knee, somewhat like the olden pipers who used a forked stick as a crutch giving the same effect. His open air recitals were his means of support for his wife and family and his professional playing always ensured the coffers were full.

During the Second World War Johnny found it easier to settle in Dublin. Although it more or less stopped his nomadic lifestyle for a while it was very fortunate for his music. At the time the Famous Piper's Club in Thomas Street was very active and Johnny Doran was a most welcome visitor there at the musical sessions. One of the members was a Clare man, John Kelly who had a shop in Capel Street, a Mecca for all traditional musicians visiting the metropolis, and Johnny was particularly welcome for John Kelly's wife was a native of County Wicklow. It was from his long friendship with the Kelly's that a chance remark by Doran to John Kelly about feeling unwell left the nation a forty minute legacy of his fine pipering. At the time Kevin Danaher was working for the "Irish Folklore Commission" at Earlsfort Terrace and from a phone call from John Kelly, invited Doran to make some recordings. This was in the Winter of 1947, just before Christmas. Johnny played ten to twelve selections in one night for the princely sum of one pound per recording.

At the end of the session Danaher made a tentative arrangement with Johnny for further recording sessions – alas, it was not to be. Around New Year's Day 1948 Johnny parked his caravan in the shelter of a high wall on a derelict site in Black Lane, near Christchurch Cathedral, near where his parents lived in New Street in the Coombe. An election was pending at the time and Johnny played at a Clann na Poblachta meeting in the Phoenix Hall and was invited to play at their final rally on the eve of the election. However four days before this event on Friday 30th January, Johnny Doran was seriously injured when part of the wall fell on his caravan smashing it to pieces. Five members of his family were injured with Johnny having to be dug from the wreckage from which he suffered spinal, head and stomach injuries. Johnny was forty years of age, a man in his prime. After a long illness and hospitalisation, Ireland's greatest Uileann piper died on 19th January 1950.

In the intervening years famous musicologists, collectors and students of Irish traditional music have examined the piping techniques of the late Johnny Doran through these now legendary recordings made by Kevin Danaher, which are still available commercially on cassette from Ceírníní Claddagh or U.C.D. Folklore Department. From the relatively short amount of recorded music and reminiscences of his friends and compatriots, it's certain that this man was a musical genius of international standing in the world of ethnic folk music.

The music lives on

The meadow has almost vanished into a concrete jungle, the piper has stopped straying but the music lingers on. Ireland has a wealth of great pipers, unfortunately, few of them now are from the Travelling Community. The one great piper from this stock is Finbar Furey, who must now play the magical music of the Uileann pipes in his own time and maybe set up a class for Travellers interested in this instrument which was once kept alive by the travelling pipers of former years. Johnny and Felix Doran gave the dance music a vitality often lacking from players of the settled community, a mode of ornamentation only gained from careful practice and understanding of the underlying rhythmical nuance of our "wild" native music. A sadness of the centuries of wanderings was evident in the playing of the slow airs especially when played on the flat set of pipes- "The Dear Irish boy", "An Chuilfhionn" played by Johnny Doran were poignant. "The Fox Chase" by Felix was a musical delight full of fun and humour as he portrayed the rustic setting, galloping horses, the frightened keen of the trapped fox with farmyard ducks and chickens cackling for good measure. Audience response was massive to this man's music with all the sounds coming from pieces of African blackwood, and Spanish cane all brought about by the bellows breathing life into a leather bag under the performer's oxter.

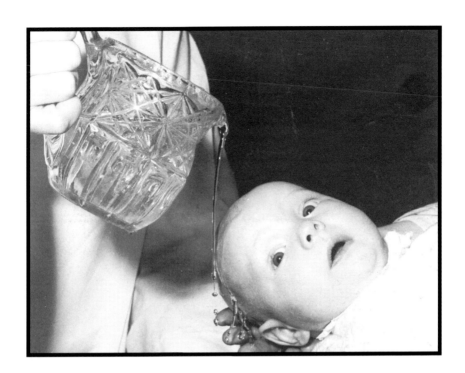

Spirituality, the faith journey of a people

Cathleen McDonagh

"Faith is very important to me, I believe God walks with me all through life."

Tammy Kiely

In order to explore the spirituality of a people I will begin by outlining what I perceive as the faith journey of a Traveller. Although the majority of Travellers are members of the Roman Catholic Church, I feel that it is important to acknowledge that there are other Christian denominations within our community. My own background is Roman Catholic and the following will reflect my own experience and research into the faith expression of the Traveller Community. I also think that it is safe to state that all Travellers, no matter what their faith, will be able to identify with the following examples of traditions and expressions of faith that are practised by Travellers who share a common history and culture.

I begin with an overview of the faith journey of a Traveller from the time of conception to the time of death. I will then go a little deeper into the faith beliefs that lie behind the practices that are lived out in a community of people. To gain an understanding of these facts is to get in touch with and gain insight into the reality of Travellers' lives. The faith expression of Travellers reflects the sense of community that expresses our way of life. The community and most immediately the family are central to the lived expression of our faith.

The Sacraments

Baptism

A child is conceived and so begins the journey of life. For the Traveller child, a blessing will be sought for the unborn child and the mother, to ensure the safe delivery of the child and the health of the mother. When the child is born its first step into the faith of its parents is to be baptised into the church. This usually takes place soon after the child is born, as parents usually wish to have their child baptised as soon as possible. The baptism is seen to benefit the child in many ways. The child is brought into the Catholic Church and gets the blessing of God. The sacrament of baptism is seen to hold both spiritual and temporal benefits which will enrich and protect the child as s/he begins her/his journey in life.

First Communion

First Holy Communion is another sacramental step on the child's faith journey. It is core to the parents' responsibility to see that their child receives their first Holy Communion. This has a very spiritual base in the faith belief of the parents. It is understood that at this stage in the child's faith journey the child is about to enter into a more physical connection and expression of their faith, to receive the body and blood of Christ. This sacrament is understood to be a sacred meeting of the child and God in the form of the host they receive at their first Holy Communion. As with baptism, core to this sacrament is the belief that as we enter into a closer relationship with God, the relationship deepens from our perspective, we draw closer to God but we don't presume to know where God stands in relation to us. We believe that we are ever present to God and that the sacraments are means of our delving deeper into the grace of God already present in our human existence. Within the sacraments we acknowledge the presence of the grace of God in our lives. We believe that this is a very active and connected presence within all that human existence holds.

Confirmation

This is a time of increasing responsibility for the child in regard to what is expected of them from their parents and their peers. Confirmation is a time of change for the child and for the parent; the child enters into a more adult-type relationship in their relationships with God and with their family. Confirmation is the sacrament of the Holy Spirit. Within this sacrament the child acknowledges the gift of the Holy Spirit in their lives. There is a deepening taking place of the child's faith relationship with God and with others.

Marriage

The sacrament of marriage is a central part of the lives of Travellers. Parents would hope to see their children marry. Within the value system of our culture, marriage would be one of the core values. In the past, a marriage would have been understood as being for life. There would not be a lot of marriage breakdown or separation. Today that has changed and there is now more marriage breakdown leading to annulments and separations. In saying this, marriage still remains a core value within our culture. Some of the customs around organising a marriage have changed. In days past matchmaking was the popular means of arranging a marriage. Today things are different; matchmaking is still in practice alongside other means of bringing about a marriage. These other means would include the young people creating their own opportunities for marriage and coming to their own decision about their life partner.

We come from a culture that centres on the family and marriage is key to family life. Most marriages will take place within the church, as we would understand the vows are taken in the eyes of God. In the past the church was the only place a marriage was understood to be valid. Today that has changed for some, but generally the marriage will take place within the church. If a union breaks down or a partner dies, a second union can be formed. Some will form a second union and others will choose not to. The main point is that marriage is a core aspect of our culture and faith practice.

Confession/Reconciliation

An insight into our faith is shown in our approach to the sacrament of reconciliation or as we would say "confession". There is within our faith an awareness of what I would call "the dark side of our humanity" in that we acknowledge the ability to sin, both within ourselves and in the world around us. God's presence is pervasive in our lives and we are very aware of it in times of trouble and on what I would call "occasions of fear".

We are a people who suffer much from injustice in our lives. There is the social injustice that we experience and all that it entails. There are also the human failings that we carry within ourselves. God is called into the centre of this experience of darkness to give forgiveness for sins and justice for people. There is an aspect of our faith that calls on God to see that justice is done, as we believe in the God of justice. We strongly believe that God will justify the innocent and the guilty will face God to answer for the wrongs they have done. We turn to the God of faith in the belief that the cries of the innocent will be heard and justified. The fact is that at times in our experience the only place Travellers believe that they are sure of receiving justice is with God. Travellers for so long have been denied access to true justice within the wider society. The God of our faith is a God who is accessible and aware of the reality of God's people.

> I think we have a very good and kind God, some people would say God is harsh because of all the wars and hunger in the world. God went through a lot of suffering for us so we could make our own decisions; we carry our own responsibility for the world. I think God is very compassionate and full of love

> (Melissa Stokes)

Pilgrimage

I went to Lourdes in thanksgiving to Our Blessed Lady. Last year I went in a wheelchair and I wasn't able to get around by myself. This year I was able to do the whole lot including the high Stations of the Cross in my bare feet and I am very thankful for that.

(Nan Maughan)

Pilgrimages are outward expressions of faith, they are prayers in the physical sense of the word. There are many reasons why people go on pilgrimage, but mostly one will go for the benefit of another. When a person goes on a pilgrimage they take a journey to a sacred place. The Reek (Croagh Patrick) is one such place of pilgrimage. This holy place of pilgrimage gives many the chance to make requests of God, to ask for help or to return in thanksgiving for an answered prayer. On this journey, people in a sense leave the world behind as they travel to their destination. The journey itself becomes a living prayer, taking time to focus on God alone within the world.

The pilgrimage is time given to God and to others. It's a journey taken in faith to a sacred place where the divine presence is felt more closely to the person. The place itself holds the sense of the sacred, in the water from a holy well or, at the grave of a person considered close to God in life. All of these places share a sense of connection to something of the sacred. There are many places that one can go to on pilgrimage but the essence of the journey is the same in all cases, that this is a very special time when we stop everything else so that we can talk to God with words and actions.

On pilgrimage we feel closer to God and it is very important to return in thanksgiving in reply to a prayer that people experience as having been granted. Three is a number that is associated with pilgrimages. A person will try to make a journey to a place of pilgrimage three times to make it complete.

Just as people go on pilgrimage for a loved one in the belief that what they do will have an effect on the well-being of that person, in a similar way that same belief is connected to healing people. To understand this belief and practice one has to know the image of God that is core to the faith of people. At the centre of these practices is the belief in a God who is accessible and present within people's existence. God is a very real presence in the lives of people. If you can see life as a journey then you will see God walks with us on this life journey.

Blessings and healing

A blessing is seen as the touch of God in a person's life, a moment that is filled with God's grace. People will call on God's blessing for themselves and others, in a very natural way, as a greeting, a prayer, or when looking at a young child. Our belief in blessings is very strong. God is called on to bless our children, the sick, the unborn and the mother. People will get vans blessed for safety in travel on the roads. Homes will be blessed so that the family will experience the grace of God within the home. There is within us a belief in the need for God's protection in this life; we seek the blessing of God all through life for everything that is connected to our lives.

Another way that we express our belief in the presence of God within the world is the practice of visiting what we would term "curing people". These are people who we believe have an ability given by God to help heal the sickness of others. Sometimes their methods will include the use of old cures that have been passed down through the generations, which will include ointments, herbal drinks and rubs. Then there are others, that people believe have the ability to heal through an act of faith, these include certain priests and religious people from all walks of life. Travellers believe that the healing power of God is accessible to these people especially in relation to the wellbeing of others.

Our Lady

The Mother of God holds a special place in the hearts of Travellers. We have a great love of Our Lady whom we see as a strong and powerful person of love and compassion. There is a deep devotion to and for the mother of God. She is understood as a friend and someone who understands the wants and needs of people. We believe and see the mother of God to be our mother who has gentleness and a strength that is called on in times of trouble and joy. As P.J. McDonagh explains, *"In the Grotto, the atmosphere was tangible by the sense of peace and prayer you could almost touch it."*

We as Travellers place great emphasis on the relationships that exist within the family and it is in this light that we see and trust the family relationship that exists between Our Lady and her son Jesus. We call on her in confidence that she will bring our prayers to the heart of Jesus. We believe that our Lady intercedes for us in life. She shares our experience of life and we believe she is always present in our human existence, as a strong and powerful expression of God's love and compassion for humanity.

The Saints

Travellers see the saints as good and holy people who, because of their love of God, have become saints. Most families will have a special saint whom they have chosen as their patron and they will feel very close to their chosen saint who in a way becomes like a good friend. The saints are called on in times of trouble and in times of hope and we pray to them to intercede on our behalf to God. The requests will include prayers for the sick to regain health, for the protection of children and for many special requests. The saints are our guides in faith and we respect and revere them as close to God and in touch with life. People will have in their possession, relics and pictures of the saints in the same way that we will have mementoes of close friends. The saints are open channels of the sacred, icons of love that intercede to God for humanity.

Death and rituals

Times of death are occasions of great sadness and we grieve within the family, as a family. There are many customs and rituals that go with times of death within our culture. The dead are always close to the living and there is a continuation between the living and the dead that survives the passing of time. There is a belief that the dead are "looking over" the living and we seek their intercession in prayer. Respect for the dead and special places of burial are part of our story. Extended families will have places of burial for the family and when someone dies no matter what the distance they will be brought, if it is possible, to this place for burial. Our Christian faith is central for us at times of death. There is a very close bond between the living and the dead and a belief that we will be united again with our loved ones who have died. The dead are passed on in memory, their story is told to the young, we hear of the events of their lives from those who knew them. Some aspect of their reality lives on in the hearts of those that loved them and those who only know them through the stories of others. The living and the dead are united in story, the dead are our family who have just passed from this life into the next, and we believe in faith that a reuniting will occur some day.

> Death is a part of who we are and what we are. It's a part of nature, a very sad and lonesome time. I believe it's not the end, it's a beginning of a new and spiritual life with God. Death is a passageway, when someone dies I grieve but I know one day we'll be reunited with each other in heaven.
>
> (Tammy Kiely)

Conclusion

The poetry of Patrick Kavanagh

For me, poets like Patrick Kavanagh capture part of the essence of the spirituality of Travellers, a spirituality that sees and discovers God in everyday events. I find in the poetry of Patrick Kavanagh a reflection of my own spirituality. His poetry reflects and speaks of the presence of God in all things. Patrick Kavanagh's mystical mind speaks of the ordinary and the sacred in life, both are one, centred within the lived experience of people. God, in Patrick's poetry, speaks to people within the mundane of everyday life. The everyday reality of people is filled with the presence of the holy.

> *And the newness that was in every stale thing*
> *When we looked at it as children: the spirit shocking*
> *Wonder in a black slanting Ulster hill*
> *Or the prophetic astonishment in the tedious talking*
> *Of an old fool will awake for us and bring*
> *You and me to the yard gate to watch the whins*
> *And the bog-holes, cart tracks, old stables where time begins.*
> (Extract from 'Advent')

The breastplate of St Patrick

This also highlights for me the mindset of the Traveller in regard to the sacred. There is completeness within this prayer that captures for me the faith of Travellers. The prayer calls on God for protection and the person praying believes that God will hear their prayer and answer in a very real and practical way. This is the belief that is behind the practice of our rituals. The presence of God walks with us and is accessible to be invoked in all things. The God of our faith is a God who is aware of all that influences our life.

I arise today,
God's strength directing me,
God's might protecting me,
God's wisdom guiding me,
God's eye looking before me,
God's ear listening to me,
God's word speaking to me,
God's hand guarding me,
God's way before me,
God's shield defending me.
(St Patrick's Breastplate- The Deer's Cry)

There is a constant dialogue with God taking place within our faith practices. To understand this one has to understand the context of our spirituality in a holistic sense. God is father and mother, creator and judge, all is connected and nothing stands alone from God.

Journey's end;
Customs around death

Anne O'Brien

A settled person's perspective

I have worked with the Travelling community since 1992. During this time I have come to form bonds with some individual Travellers and share a solidarity with the Traveller community itself whose right I believe it is to live as equals in this country and to be recognised as a distinct ethnic group by Irish society.

Facing death – my personal encounters with loss

Before I began my work with the Parish of the Travelling People, death and grief were a familiar part of my personal story and featured a little in my working life. I have also been privileged to accompany a few people during their last journey from this life. The attendance at funerals, being present with people in their grief, ritualising with and for others have been part of my life's experience. I feel that I've looked death in the face and am open to helping other people do likewise, as it seems more wholesome and healthy to do so. Yet, I am afraid of death, it still scares me, and remains in the shadows as something that is untouchable and unknowable.

These were and are my entry-points in approaching Travellers with their losses and grief. When I think of death and the Traveller Community two areas of thought predominate; namely the high "rates of morbidity" among this community in comparison with the settled population and the ways in which this distinct cultural group grieve and mourn their dead.

I have witnessed and been present at people's losses and at the deaths and funerals of others. In recalling these deaths, I remember; a woman who lost two adult sons amongst other tragedies, parents who lost children to metabolic disorders, a man whose wife had died after a long illness, others who had miscarriages and still births, a young girl whose dad died tragically and an adult woman who still grieves for the loss of her mother. Some of these people I had accompanied to Lourdes in their journey of hope, seeking comfort and cures.

In conveying a sense of my encounters with death as experienced by this community sound, image and emotion reverberate:- hearing the wailing sound of the great grief cries echoing the intense lonesomeness of this pain and loss; feeling a palpable bleakness or fatality surrounding death and images of the dark predominate in visualising the reality of death itself.

These responses may also be similar when anyone encounters the human face of death and the ritualisation of loss. Yet I believe that the Traveller community have been acutely exposed to this dark face of death, unlike other groups in our society.

Causes of death in the Traveller community – the tragic reality

The facts speak for themselves. Travellers have higher "rates of morbidity" for all causes of death but the incidences of death are significantly higher among Travellers for accidents; metabolic disorders; respiratory ailments and congenital problems.

In addition to this

◆ Travellers have more than double the natural rate of still births.

◆ Infant mortality rates are three times higher than the national rate.

◆ Only 1 in 20 live over the age of 50.

◆ Traveller men live on average 10 years less than settled men.

◆ Traveller women live on average 12 years less than settled women.

The long dark shadow of discrimination

These facts reflect the unjust reality of Travellers being forced to live their lives in a context of racial discrimination, exclusion and marginalisation. In this culture, Traveller parents need to rear their children in a way that allows them to survive in a society which is oppressive:

> These factors inevitably have a negative effect on physical and mental health and require more than personal, social or health services to alleviate them
> (*Travellers' Health and Accommodation Statistics in the Coolock Area, 1994*)

Consequently, multiple deaths and fatal tragedies confront this community, as a result of policies and actions initiated by the dominant settled institutions and by society as a whole. Our collective participation in, and responsibility for, the racism and discrimination experienced by the Traveller community, mirrors the dark side of both ourselves and Irish society.

Ireland today seems to survive or succeed by the urge to dominate "the other", namely the different, the non-conformist, the excluded:

More alarmingly, we persecute the others all around us – anyone who threatens our precariously established identity.

(Mary Condren 1999)

Indeed this darkness reflects our negative nature which can be "displaced unto others who act as scapegoats, allowing us to wallow in our own self-righteousness," (Condren 1999). The Traveller community carry the projections, distortions and pathologies of "the other" for the majority sedentary population in our society. All of these factors contribute to the experience of death by the Traveller community.

When I stood at the removal of the body of a Traveller woman's adult son, I stood as someone who cherishes, knows this woman and shares in her pain of yet another tragic loss. But I also stood as a settled woman bearing witness to a legacy of multiple tragedies experienced by her community and feeling ashamed of this reality. This shame is echoed in a similar way when I encounter scenes from Northern Ireland, Bosnia, Rwanda, Kosovo or Chechnya. I feel outrage at what we as settled people are collectively "doing to" the Traveller community. This needs to be acknowledged and confronted by us. I, as an individual working with Travellers have stood in the presence of the oppression experienced by this community which finds at times its starkest expression in the darkness of death.

Nomadism and death

We have seen that nomadism is central to the Traveller community's way of life and it is key to the worldview of being a Traveller. Nomadism is a mindset reflected in the bonds of kinship which are at the heart of how this community experiences its identity and organises and structures itself. Travellers' experience of bereavement and the customs associated with it express the close family ties, extended family bonds and religious and folk beliefs of this distinct culture. Death threatens the survival of this community. It breaks up the close-knit ties, so all from far and near gather in solidarity around the dead person, to make sure that those ties are not completely broken. Travelling is only part of what it means to be nomadic. Yet travelling enables some Travellers to come to terms with death. As this community is more restricted in their mobility due to social laws and attitudes, traditional coping and support systems which are essential to grieving for the Traveller community could also be threatened. This factor could in turn diminish and threaten the nomadic nature of these people which is the core to their ethnicity and identity.

Open expressions of grieving – ritualising chaos

Travellers grieve openly with an intense rawness that is externalised in a physical and loud manner. This is good, wholesome and necessary. Such open expressions of grieving have been replaced by a perhaps more sanitised, hidden or a more supposed, "dignified" stance of the settled population. Death has been described as an experience of chaos and crisis. Sometimes I wonder if the settled community has tried to ritualise this chaos into apparent order while Travellers and other nomadic groups have allowed their ritual to express the chaotic and critical experience of death?

Embracing "the dark" – Traveller rituals surrounding death

Whatever the causes of death or negative forces affecting it, the Traveller community has a rich body of ritual and customs which helps to ritualise the grieving process. Ireland as a whole, regardless of change in religious attitudes seems to embrace and enact ritual at all key rites of passage.

However, from my experience the Traveller community hold's a core body of ritual (some of which resembles that of Ireland years ago and of today, rooted in the Celtic tradition, some of a perhaps more traditional society where death threatens the group and its culture) which is healthy, for the grieving process. In using the image of 'the dark' in another way, it seems to me that Travellers more freely embrace the dark side of individual and communal experience by the way they embrace and ritualise death.

This is not to put Traveller customs surrounding death on a pedestal or to romanticise them or to deny features common to all cultures. Rather it is to say that their core body of ritual has something for us to learn from and to be renewed by.

Rituals at the time of death

The specific customs Travellers have before, during and after burial embody a great respect for and honouring of the dead. These customs include:-

◆ Travelling far and wide for funerals; the great speed at which news of a death travels (not by media), there is also the possibility of fasting at the time of a funeral.

◆ The opening and re-opening of the coffin, much touching and kissing of the dead person. Approaching the coffin often and talking to the dead person aloud, during the Mass etc. Relics and coins may be placed in the coffin, pieces of the dead person's hair and other keepsakes are valued by the bereaved. Loud, externalisation of sorrow as discussed earlier, the grief is open and demonstrative.

◆ Sparing no expense with the coffin and funeral crosses.

◆ Wreaths, flowers, statues given by all, rarely mass cards

◆ Drinking by some families to anaesthetise the pain and perhaps to help talk about the dead. Much talking and story-telling shared by the bereaved during these days.

◆ Burial is usually in the place of origin of the family group, particularly where the mother's or father's people are buried. Each family group or clan from a particular area use undertakers, priests and churches known to those families.

Rituals in the year after burial

These rituals may include:

◆ **Moving on from the place where the family lived,** to cope with the loss, perhaps temporarily. Some burn a trailer and belongings to free the spirit of the dead person and to cope with the intense pain of remembering or with memories associated with the person (see similarities with Aboriginal culture in Michelle Dunne's research, 1998). This is not as common a practice as before.

◆ **Photographs of the dead and other keepsakes** adorn many trailers and homes, keeping the memory alive.

◆ **The ninth day** – this is the day when many believe the soul leaves the body. A Mass and visiting of the grave happens on this day. This is a difficult day for the family.

◆ **Month's masses** – some have Masses said every month for a year and gather at the grave but others honour the first month or the Month's Mind, after the person's death.

◆ **The blessing of the cross or crossing ceremony** – A year after the person dies, the headstone is erected and blessed, some have a Mass beforehand. About as many people gather as did at the funeral; all travel again from far and wide. The feelings of grief may be as raw and intense on this day as they were when the person died and was buried.

◆ **The blessing of the graves, or pattern, or cemetery Sunday** – is honoured by Travellers. Most visit the grave often enough throughout the year, particularly during November. Many buy special things for the grave, small statues from places like Lourdes.

◆ **Prayers and poetry, words of remembrance, offered for the dead,** often gathered and written in publications by the bereaved families.

Some of these rituals are not common to all Traveller family group-ings. Some are particular to individual families. Some of these rituals have connections with the customs of settled culture and the Celtic tradition and many of them are shared with other nomadic peoples. These rituals attempt to externalise the darkness of grief and the grieving process. By embracing death in such a wholesome way Traveller culture has much to offer others, as it is "only by moving fully into the darkness can we move through it into the light" (*Shaki Gawain in Mary Paula Walsh 1995*).

Climbing the heights of love; a Traveller woman's faith journey

Colm Kilcoyne

Margaret Lawrence set out from Ballina to climb Croagh Patrick on the Thursday 7th December 1995. She fell and died on the mountain. She was buried in Ballina the following Tuesday. Margaret was a Traveller, twenty-nine years old and single. She made the Pilgrimage for her young niece, Sharon Mariosa, who was ill.

St. Nicholas special school in Ballina is for children with mental handicap. Some are moderate, others severely handicapped, more are autistic children. Margaret worked with the autistic children.

Margaret herself had a brother, seven years younger than her, who is severely handicapped. She brought him to the school on his very first day. Her parents would have lost several children, some as babies. One sister of Margaret's died in a fire twenty years ago.

Margaret went to St. Nicholas on six months work experience, ten years ago. Ruth McNeela was on the staff. "She was out on her own. She had this huge capacity to be with a child, to befriend that child and stay loving it in its worst tantrums. Never in ten years did I see her lose her temper or show frustration. She had a capacity to keep loving, to be present right through the storm. Margaret said very little but she could see ahead of any of us into the minds and emotions of the children. Take two of our children, Lisa and Colm. Lisa had cerebral palsy, Colm was autistic. He could be very difficult. Lisa liked Colm. Margaret saw this and quietly facilitated the friendship. She helped each find a beauty in their lives by treating them both as precious young children. This was her gift.

Since September '95 Margaret had been dealing on a one-to-one basis with Caroline, spending all her time with her, going to the shops and getting her ready for the day when she'd have to leave the school. Caroline could be troublesome. But she adored Margaret.

Margaret Lawrence was slim, fair, funny and would have loved children of her own. That is not the way it worked out. Instead, the children in St. Nicholas got her love. She refused offers to represent Travellers on communities and organisations, partly because she was shy, partly because she believed she was herself before she was representative of any one group of people. Her skills with children meant other group homes in the service tried to entice her away but she didn't want to move. "I'm happy here, with the children," was the answer.

She wrote poetry. Everyone who left the school got one of Margaret's poems, specially written for the occasion.

Margaret Lawrence was spiritual but not holy, not pious. She especially liked the bidding prayers at school masses because these prayers were close to the pain of the children and their parents. Pain she understood. Ruth McNeela said "She saw straight into your pain. You just knew it. She never spoke about it but you sensed she was looking into your heart. The children understood this as well".

Some have said climbing Croagh Patrick in the dark dead of winter was a relapse into pishogues, a spasm from her Travelling background. This is not true. I once heard a Traveller retell the story of the Bible as a series of stories about travelling. The wandering Adam and Eve after the garden, the Jews in Egypt, the various exiles and the return home, the journey of Mary and Joseph to Bethlehem, the wandering of Jesus through the towns and villages of the holy land. The road to Calvary – the journey home to the Father. Told that way, the Bible is the story of a travelling people. A pilgrim people.

Here and there, on the road, there are places where the presence of God is sensed more powerfully. At wells that draw life from the depths, mountains that call down energy from the heights, places dense with the pain and longing of pilgrims who have stopped to feel the healing presence of their God. Travellers all know these holy places and holy wells.

Croagh Patrick is one such place. You travel up to travel in. You walk on stones made smooth by 1,000 years of penance in the hope that the exercise will smooth whatever is jagged and hurt in your heart.

By climbing the Reek Travellers believe they come closer to God physically. God is to be found within the journey. The journey itself becomes the prayer. "I love climbing the Reek, it's a hard climb alright but it's worth it. I feel better in myself, it's a good thing to do and I feel closer to God after it" said one Traveller man. It's the most natural thing in the world for Travellers to go to Croagh Patrick to pray for some intention. Only this year, on St. Patrick's day, one of Margaret's cousins went with two of his young sons to initiate them into the tradition of the Reek.

Margaret Lawrence hired a car from Ballina to the foot of Croagh Patrick. Then she made her pilgrimage. Then she made her pilgrimage alone. Ruth McNeela insists that it was not for a miracle or a cure. "Margaret wasn't like that. She'd never ask God to do tricks. No, she climbed as much for her own strength as for the young girl's recovery."

Her intention was to do the climb three times. The Biblical three. No-one knows if she did them all. Only that she slipped on the cold, wet and treacherous summit of the Reek, fell and died.

Margaret Lawrence crossed the divide between Traveller and settled to the point where she was a bit of both but not fully either. This caused her pain. The day of her funeral mass one of the bidding prayers said that she was a teacher, a pilgrim and a Traveller. Now, the prayer went on, her unique and loving spirit has travelled home to God.

Part 2

Challenges from the Traveller community

A new response or the same old story?

David Joyce

Money is not the issue!

In trying to address the accommodation issues that currently concern Travellers the crisis that exists could never be described in terms of a lack of funding or resources to meet the accommodation needs. For many years the government has made the necessary finance requirements available to local authorities. However, this money has not always been drawn down by the relevant bodies.

In this chapter, I will try to examine the influence of official accommodation policy over the last thirty- five years. I would also like to explore what I see as being a paradox of policy between the intention of national government and the actual practice of the local authorities in the delivery of accommodation at local level. In addition to this, I will also try to outline what will be the major challenges for Travellers in terms of accommodation in the future. While these challenges have been influenced by the policy and practice of the last thirty years, they also have been, and continue to be, created by changes in attitude among Travellers to their accommodation requirements. The major social changes that have affected Travellers need to be examined before the challenges regarding accommodation can be met. In addressing the issue of accommodation, the changing role and importance of nomadism for Travellers also needs to be looked at.

Changes in accommodation policy

The 1960's – a policy of isolation not assimilation

In the late 1960s the State for the first time began, through local authorities, to make Traveller accommodation officially available in the form of halting sites and later group housing. The accommodation of Travellers in standard local authority dwellings had always been part of on-going general accommodation programmes. Travellers who wished to access standard housing did, and continue, to suffer from discriminatory allocation practices within local authorities, although some Travellers were being housed prior to the 1960s. The practice of providing specific forms of accommodation for Travellers in the guise of halting sites, hard -stands and later group housing, only began following the publication of the first major government report on Travellers, *The Report of the Commission on Itinerancy 1963.*

The main thrust of the report, which did not involve any consultation with Travellers, has been described as a policy of *assimilation.* However the policy regarding accommodation which emerged at a local level following its publication, I believe can only be mistakenly described as *isolationist*, as the actual physical locations of halting sites provided by local authorities could only lead to isolation for Travellers. Even though halting sites were seen by *The Report of Commission on Itinerancy 1963* as a temporary measure to enable Travellers to progress into "housing", the practice of discrimination which existed within local authorities towards housing allocation to Travellers meant, that whatever notion the state might have had about assimilation, it would never be put into practice at a local level. Given local councils record, even Travellers who "wanted" to assimilate would never get the opportunity.

What began to develop at local level was a "policy of isolation". The lack of vision and or imagination in regard to the design and quality of halting sites and their physical remoteness from other accommodation/housing areas, meant that they were never intended to meet the basic needs of Travellers as human beings never mind their specific needs relating to nomadism or Traveller identity.

The "policy of isolation" operated by local authorities had two effects on Travellers. Firstly, the poor quality and remote location of accommodation detached Travellers from settled institutions like schools and other social services. Secondly, employment in "settled" work places and the limited degree of social interaction that Travellers living on the roadside had with settled people were also reduced.

The rules and regulations required of tenants on halting sites meant that Travellers were also increasingly being isolated from structures in the Traveller Community as it became increasing difficult to maintain family connections, to pursue economic activity and to create social interaction among families. Travellers who try to continue some form of economic activity, in Traveller specific accommodation, immediately become identified as "problem tenants". Likewise, Travellers who allow family members to share bays or to double-up also create a problem. The effect that the notion of Travellers as "problem tenants" has had on local authorities has been to continue to isolate Travellers from residential areas. The actions of councils, influenced by opposition from settled people, has resulted in the adoption of a policy that is the opposite of an assimilationist policy, whereby Traveller specific accommodation continues to be kept away from the "normal".

The provision that has been made for Travellers by local authorities over the last thirty years has been quite haphazard and in very few areas has Traveller accommodation been actively or willingly proposed by councils. Provision has only come about because conditions had become so extreme.

The Report of the Task Force on the Travelling Community 1995

A policy with direction

The change in national policy on Traveller accommodation over the last five years has been remarkable. This change has largely resulted from the publication of *The Report of the Task Force on the Travelling Community 1995*. To go from a position where the existing policy had no real direction or framework for implementation, to the introduction of a specific piece of legislation on Traveller accommodation is unique. Despite the fact that the legislation is still weak on definite implementation structures and despite concerns in regard to the local authority retaining the main responsibility for provision of accommodation, local authorities are nevertheless obliged to adopt Traveller accommodation programmes for specific periods of time which allow at least for some measure of development on accommodation provision.

Recognition of the cultural rights of Travellers

The language and trust of the Task Force recommendations marked a major change from previous government reports. The acknowledgement of the cultural rights of Travellers can been seen in the wording of many of the recommendations of the report. Traveller representatives were involved in and played a key part in the development of the Task Force recommendations, through the involvement of organisations like Irish Traveller Movement, Pavee Point and others.

While it is quite easy to point out the over- riding direction of *The Commission on Itinerancy Report 1963* and to a certain extent that of *The Report of the Review Body 1983*, toward assimilation. The policy direction of *The Report of the Task Force 1995* can best be described as one aimed at inclusion arising out of cultural respect. The structures and initiatives that have been created following the Task Force report deal with Travellers in mainstream services such as Health, Education etc. and the economy through social economy measures. Already the government departments responsible for these areas have put in place pilot measures and structures to meet the recommendations.

Accommodating nomadism

The official provision of Traveller accommodation over the last thirty-five years has done little to acknowledge the right of Travellers to practice a nomadic existence. Whilst the nature and pattern of travelling has changed in the last thirty years, nomadism has always been a defining characteristic of Travellers who have had a tradition of moving which is related to their economic needs and to reasons of family and culture. The Task Force in addressing the issue of accommodation promotes respect for Travellers' nomadic heritage. The response to this from government has been the promotion of policy that intends to meet the need for appropriate accommodation which attempts to "accommodate" nomadism.

However the responsibility for the implementation of this policy of "respect for culture" still rests in the hands of local authorities. It will be interesting to see how a local statutory structure, which in practice has gone in the opposite direction to the stated government policy over the last thirty -five years (i.e. in regard to the policy of assimilation), will respond to this new direction in policy. Will the result be the same in that local authorities will continue to defy government policy by creating accommodation programmes at local level that continue to isolate Travellers?

The development of a Traveller Accommodation Strategy

Following *The Report of the Task Force of the Travelling Community 1995*, the Department of the Environment produced a Traveller Accommodation Strategy in response to the recommendation relating to accommodation. The strategy was described by the Department as being "a framework within which the needs of Travellers for suitable accommodation are met." The key elements of the strategy were:

◆ The introduction of specific legislation on Traveller Accommodation.

◆ The establishment of a Unit within the Department to co-ordinate a programme for Traveller accommodation.

◆ The establishment of a National Traveller Accommodation Consultative Group to advise the Minister on accommodation issues.

The Housing (Traveller Accommodation) Act 1998

The main provisions

The Housing (Traveller Accommodation) Act was enacted in July 1998. Again the Act has been described by the Department of the Environment as a legislative framework to facilitate the implementation of the Government's commitments in relation to meeting the accommodation needs of Travellers.

The main provisions of *The Housing (Traveller Accommodation) Act 1998* are, to:

◆ Provide for the preparation and adoption by relevant housing authorities of five-year programmes for the provision Traveller accommodation to meet both the existing and projected need for the period of the plan.

◆ Provide for the establishment by local authorities of Local Traveller Accommodation committees to facilitate consultation with Travellers/ Traveller organisations on the preparation and implementation of Traveller accommodation programmes.

◆ Provide for public consultation process in respect of the preparation of accommodation programmes including the opportunity to comment on draft programmes.

◆ Provide for the establishment of a National Traveller Accommodation Consultative Committee on a statutory basis to advise the Minister on any general aspect of Traveller Accommodation.

◆ Require housing authorities to take reasonable steps to secure the implementation of Traveller Accommodation Programmes for their areas.

Other provisions of the Act change planning legislation to include the objectives of accommodation programmes into county development plans and the extension of previous provisions made in *The Housing Act 1997* to Traveller halting sites. This provision relates to the control of anti-social behaviour by tenants (Travellers) on local authority-managed accommodation.

Consulting with Travellers in providing Traveller-specific accommodation

The needs that Travellers have in terms of accommodation are very basic. When Travellers are on the move they are simply looking for somewhere they can pull in that is safe from the traffic and which would ideally have the basics of water and toilets. Travellers aren't mad – they don't want to park in dangerous areas or to attract trouble and like everyone they want to keep their children safe. Travellers are not looking for anything elaborate; all they want is access to basic facilities and freedom from harassment from the authorities.

There have been some improvements made by local authorities in the last couple of years who are now realising that it is particularly necessary to consult Travellers in regard to the design and layout of the accommodation being provided for them. A number of schemes have been provided around the country that have been successful in this regard. What is happening now in the building of sites is that Traveller accommodation is becoming a mixture of halting sites and housing schemes and these are in some way combined , which would be the preference of many Travellers.

When you are talking about accommodating transient Travellers you are talking in terms of lay-bys, like the ones that Travellers used in the past. At present, there is a lot of road building going on and if you were to incorporate lay-bys into these new structures over the next few years there would be adequate space to make provision for transient Travellers. In the next few years authorities are going to have lots of opportunities, in term of the road building, to find space that could be used in very appropriate ways by Travellers. It just takes a little imagination on the part of the authorities to face this issue.

There are three categories of Traveller specific accommodation, which are recommended to meet the distinct needs of Travellers.

(i)   group housing schemes

These are purpose-built schemes which provide houses / bungalows for Traveller families who are interested in being accommodated in this way

(ii)   permanent halting sites

These are permanent structures with individual bays and a permanent structure which incorporate kitchen, toilet and shower with hot and cold water.

(iii)   transient sites

These are halting sites for Travellers who are on the move and who are stopping for a short period of time- these sites should consist of running water, electricity, toilets and refuse collection.

Of the Traveller population in Ireland, about one third live in houses and see themselves as being settled in an area. Another third live in local authority- provided halting sites, and the remaining Travellers are living on illegal encampments or on unofficial sites

In drawing up and designing Local Traveller Accommodation Programmes, *The Housing (Traveller Accommodation) Act 1998* requires local authorities to reflect the real need for a range of Traveller accommodation options which include those mentioned above. The recognition of this range of accommodation which needs to be provided in regard to transient halting sites in particular, gives important legal recognition to the nomadic identity of Travellers. It is important that in the implementation of this recognition that innovative ways to meet the needs of Travellers who move more regularly are found. This provision of the Act becomes negative if we see the transient sites as 'reservations' that control and have the effect of restricting the movement of Travellers.

Accommodating nomadism

One of the greatest difficulties for the local authorities dealing with Traveller families is understanding the concept of a nomadism. The only response from local authorities in relation to nomadism is one of preventing it rather than seriously trying to come to terms with this mind-set and accommodating it. I am of the opinion that when it comes to the area of nomadism local authorities cannot understand it at all in relation to Traveller accommodation.

Many Traveller families are on the move either because they want to or because of work. When considering Traveller accommodation the extended family is very important. The sense of belonging to a group, of recognising and identifying with that group is important to Travellers. This is particularly important when extended families want to be accommodated together. The local authority in charge of housing for many Travellers only deals with individuals and so families are split up. These families then find themselves in a housing estate of two to three hundred houses and they soon feel very isolated. This is the reason why many Travellers move out of houses when they are allocated to them. That is the price they have to pay to hold onto the extended family.

I was quite happy when I was living in a caravan in the group-housing scheme. I didn't have a house there but I had services and my family around and that suited me. Moving onto a site would have been a similar experience because the services provided would have been the same. When I moved into a house I felt more isolated because I didn't have many people around. For Travellers, this sense of isolation can be a stronger reason to change accommodation than when the actual level of provision of services are poor. This is not to say however that we are not obliged to provide good quality accommodation for Travellers. In particular in the year 2000 the choice to have good quality accommodation is one that many Travellers would like to have. This is what Travellers need and want, and it is also what they are entitled to.

This legislation, for the first time, acknowledges nomadism and the right to move and provides some legal protection for nomadism. How this legislation is interpreted and implemented at a local level will be important regarding its effect on Travellers.

Abuse of Section 32 – a cause of concern

While the main response to the Traveller Accommodation Act from Traveller groups has been positive, Section 32 of the Act, which increases the powers of eviction already available to local authorities, is of major concern for Travellers. The already flagrant use and abuse of this section by local authorities highlights what may be the real intentions of local authorities toward Traveller accommodation, which could be the minimalist provision and maximum harassment of families in need of either permanent or transient accommodation. So far, many local authorities have used these powers extensively to evict Travellers while at the same time they have put little effort into providing a place for the 1200 Traveller families on the roadside. The use of extra powers without acting on other provisions of the legislation is a tell-tale sign that little has changed yet in the mindset of council officials to Traveller accommodation.

Response of local councillors to the Act

There has been a mixed response, on behalf of councillors, to the Act itself. On the one hand they have been extremely cautious to interpret the Act in the best way to try and get Travellers involved. In some cases, Councils have involved Traveller representatives in the actual preparation of the reports and allowed them, along with other residents, to have input into the actual writing of the report. On the other hand, there have been situations where Traveller representatives and members of the local community were told they couldn't even see the reports until they went public. Unfortunately, the majority of Councils fitted into this more negative category.

Obstacles to Traveller accommodation – hostility and prejudice in Irish society

Boulders: symbols of oppression

Local authorities for a long time have been involved in bouldering up or blocking off areas where families had been camping, but it has recently become pre-emptive on a large scale. These boulders have become a symbol of oppression because they are a direct attack on the nomadic lifestyle of Travellers. They are a physical manifestation of local authorities' anti-Traveller policies. Many traditional places have been blocked off, leaving families to move into areas where there may be a problem. The in-fill of the capital and the lack of land availability are also making it much harder for Travellers to find places. As soon as families move off a piece of land the local authorities will move in with bulldozers. Travellers are not going to go away and the situation is not going to be resolved by forcing Travellers into other areas.

In some cases, private individuals have done things themselves to deny land to Travellers. They might dig up the side of a road and put down boulders and the local authorities will turn a blind eye to it when, in other circumstances ,they would be prosecuted under planning or litter laws. There have been cases of Travellers looking for money to move on. I would not condone that, but there have also been cases where builders have encouraged Travellers to come onto land, paying them to do so in the belief that their application for planning permission for change of land use will then be speeded up. The current situation has encouraged this kind of behaviour on both sides.

Obviously Travellers seeking land and meeting such official hostility can be driven to some form of protest. I think they are perfectly entitled to engage in that. They are forced into it in many cases. In a sense they have no other choice. But very few incidents have happened. When you think about the potential for real unrest, Travellers have been very tolerant and long-suffering.

Prejudice: the main obstacle to Traveller accommodation

The main obstacle to the provision of adequate accommodation has in large part to do with opposition based on prejudice from the settled community. When a site for Travellers is proposed in an area, residents groups are formed overnight to oppose it and this is blatant discrimination. The actual physical building of a site and the provision of money in terms of resources from the Department of the Environment aren't really a hindrance and lack of funding for Traveller accommodation has never been an issue. The money has always been available, but at the end of the day it's all down to the people at local level.

With the increase in the small number of asylum seekers and refugees in the last few years, there is a perception in Ireland that racism is something new. Travellers have been experiencing racism for generations. At the end of the second millennium, Travellers are still very much outcasts in Irish society. The negative images of Travellers affect the confidence and pride, of young Travellers in particular, in their own identity and community.

Another reason why good quality accommodation is not provided is a lack of will on the part of local authorities, local councils and officials to stand up to opposition from local residents. It's easier to let people live for years with the very low standards and in many cases with no access to water, toilets etc. than to actually make a stand and probably make yourself unpopular with many residents. Politicians or local officials would see this type of situation as difficult, but to me it is just a human decision to be made in regard to the provision of water and services.

There are attitudes towards Travellers and Traveller accommodation and for me it is strange and incomprehensible that many people are quite prepared to allow or at least to tolerate people living in very hard circumstances. There is the hope that if they don't give Travellers proper services they will move away after a while. It only serves to benefit both Travellers and settled people for proper services to be provided and we all need to call on councillors to make tough decisions.

Challenges for the future

- *Members of the Traveller community and of Traveller organisations* are challenged to further develop the collective views of

Travellers to feed into the consultative processes envisaged under the *Housing (Traveller Accommodation) Act 1998*. These groups must also contribute to the innovative thinking that is needed in order to address the accommodation needs of Travellers, particularly those who move more regularly.

- *Local development groups.*

Those involved in local development are challenged to see Traveller accommodation as a local development issue. Having good and appropriate accommodation is a prerequisite to other development. Those involved in local development can play a role in building the capacity for involvement of Travellers and Traveller organisations. They can also play a role in being persuaders for, and supporters of the need for an appropriate Traveller accommodation programme.

- *Local Authority Officials.*

Local Authority officials have a key role in bringing forward proposals for Traveller accommodation. It is vital that they embrace the positive understanding of Traveller culture including its nomadic aspects. They must also be supportive of collective processes in the Traveller community and give recognition to the work that is done by Traveller organisations in their areas.

- *Political representatives.*

Finally, political representatives are challenged to show leadership in both presenting a positive understanding of the Traveller community and by committing themselves to the processes outlined in the *Housing (Traveller Accommodation) Act 1998*.

My hopes for the future

I think the promise the government made five years ago that by the year 2000 all Travellers would be accommodated in the accommodation of their choice is nowhere near being fulfilled. There has only been 123 Traveller specific units of accommodation provided, whether it's sites or group housing, which falls very short of the 3000 promised. It still remains a wish however that I hope will become a reality with the introduction of the next five- year programme to come into effect in March 2000. By the time it finishes it will be the year 2004.

In general, my hope for the new millennium is that Travellers will become more active at a local level all around the country especially in regard to addressing accommodation issues, but also in regard to addressing other issues which affect Travellers. The Equal Status Legislation that will come into effect will give Travellers the opportunity to do this. People will have a type of protection, will be more free to make their voices heard and will have the support of the *Housing (Traveller Accommodation) Act 1998*.

Still waiting in hope

Pat Brady

Task Force Recommendations

> The Task Force recommends the provision of 3100 units of accommodation by the year 2000
>
> Task Force Report (DR.1.) 1995.

> A network of permanent sites is required across the country. A network of transient sites is required across the country and in each local authority area
>
> (DR.7.)

Up to November 1998 a total of 123 Traveller specific units of accommodation were provided. This amounts to an average of about 40 per annum across the whole of Ireland. Faced with this huge disparity between what was promised, and what was in fact delivered, I feel compelled to ask the question "Why?". For some ideas which might assist in answering this question, I will refer to the excellent study, *Accommodating Travelling People* (1996), written for CROSSCARE by Dr. Kieran McKeown with the assistance of Ms. Bríd McGrath. Most of the conclusions of this Report, although directly related to the Dublin Diocese are nevertheless valid and have much to offer in understanding the present situation in regard to Traveller Accommodation.

CROSSCARE Report: Reasons for failure to implement plan

> The failure of the 1986 plan of Dublin County Council can be attributed to specific identifiable defects in the means adopted by local and central administration for dealing with the Task
>
> *CROSSCARE, 1996*

The study goes on to show that while local opposition is always identified as the main problem to the construction of sites nevertheless, sites have been developed despite this opposition. If this is in fact the case, why then have local authorities produced even less units of accommodation in the years subsequent to the *Report of the Task Force 1995* and CROSSCARE Reports, than in the years previous?

1. Lack of core planners and lack of commitment

"There has been a failure to develop a corps of planners and administrators". Too often civil servants do not stay long enough to become acquainted with the brief and to build a positive relationship with Travellers and their support organisations before moving to another department. The situation raises doubts about the commitment of senior local authority administrators to the delivery of Traveller specific accommodation, with all that involves. Indeed the recent plans for Traveller accommodation from several local authorities for the next five years only serve to confirm this scepticism.

2. Lack of Traveller involvement in decision - making

Despite being in operation for almost a year, the recommendation of the Traveller Accommodation Act that local authorities set up consultative committees with Traveller participation has not been fully realised and the experience has been that the level of Traveller involvement has been minimal and indications show that, as far as Travellers are concerned, this is a policy decision made by many local councils.

One searches in vain for real signs of progress or for a desire for real participation or for enthusiasm for the task in hand. This in turn produces a very negative attitude from Travellers and we are back in a vicious circle of mistrust on all sides.

3. Refusal to take Traveller culture (notably nomadism and the Traveller economy) into account in providing accommodation

The fact that a number of Traveller families move from one place to another is a characteristic of nomadism. The fact that these and other families engage in a variety of economic activities around trading is another core element of Traveller life. "The culture and identity of Travellers is to be recognised and taken into account". (*Task Force, BR1*)

This is the fundamental statement of *The Report of the Task Force on the Travelling Community 1995*. Yet most new five-year plans specifically discuss "our families" or "indigenous families" (i.e. Traveller families must have lived in the local council area for some years) and specifically exclude Traveller economic activities in all proposed new developments.

While accepting that nomadism and the economic activities of Travellers are seen as a problem by many people, the way forward is not to deny Travellers two of the most fundamental elements of their culture and way of life. Attempts to do so have failed miserably in the past and will continue to fail in the future. Perhaps we could decide, as a nation facing an intercultural challenge in the new millennium, that the way forward is not to insist that all people of different cultures, religions, and / or ethnic backgrounds, whether they have been a part of Irish society for centuries (as Travellers have been) or, whether they are coming into the country, must do it "our way" or not at all. To do so would be to deny our growth and progress as a nation in the area of interculturalism.

4. Perceived shortcomings at central Government level

The *CROSSCARE Report* identified serious problems at central Government level. I can only conclude, however, from what I have seen that much of this is no longer true. The government has provided,

◆ a new Traveller Accommodation unit

◆ finance

◆ a new act

◆ a draft of policy documents

◆ a National Consultative Committee that is real and active

among the many positive responses that have occurred.

5. Ultimate failure lies in the hands of local authorities

The focus, therefore, returns once more to the local situation. Despite all the "back up" from Central government, local authorities nationwide fail miserably in the provision of Traveller specific

Accommodation. One is left to wonder what it takes to resolve this issue of accommodating Travelling people.

Suggestions for improvements

The *CROSSCARE Report* suggested that, in order to improve the present unsatisfactory situation,

◆ the existing arrangements in regard to local authorities would be ammended

◆ a body which *the Task Force* also describes as a National Traveller Accommodation Agency whose sole function would be to ensure that Travellers were given a decent, safe place to live, would be established.

Given that the national output of Traveller Accommodation has dropped from 90 per annum (1986 – 1996) to 40+ per annum (1996 – 1998) the issue seems to cry out for a new approach.

The attitudes of settled people in regard to Traveller accommodation

Travellers are a distinct cultural and ethnic group in Ireland constituting less than 1% of the total population. There are currently about 5000 Travelling families totalling some 30,000 individuals of whom more than 50% are under 15 years of age. Since more than 3500 of these families are currently living in a variety of permanent and temporary accommodation types of varying standards, there is less than 1500 families requiring Traveller specific accommodation.

One of the unique features of the *CROSSCARE Report* was its attempt to assess the attitudes and emotions felt by settled people towards Travellers. The attitudes of the settled community have long been used as a reason why local authorities have been unable to meet their responsibilities. *CROSSCARE* asked AGB Adelaide and a market Research Company to do a Report for us inquiring into the attitudes and emotions of settled people towards Travellers. Just under 600 people were interviewed in the Dublin Diocesan area.

The clear experience of Travellers is of almost universal exclusion from mainstream life in Ireland. Yet, despite this hostility, as experienced by Travellers, a relatively high percentage of settled people when interviewed in their own homes expressed positive attitudes towards Travellers. "There is clearly an underlying acceptance that Travellers have not been well treated and that they have rights that should be respected." (*CROSSCARE 1996*). However, when the issue of accommodation for Travellers arises locally there is an almost universal refusal to allow it to go ahead. Although settled people are, in theory, sympathetic to the accommodation needs of Travellers, when faced with the prospect of Travellers living in their area/estate, a very strong negative reaction is evoked. There is a certain "Not in my backyard" attitude that is prevalent among settled people.

Travellers are in a "no win" situation. As long as there is a shortfall of well over 1200 units of accommodation Travellers have no place to settle. On the other hand, when Travellers settle on unofficial sites local communities will object. The anger of local communities is turned to Travellers not to the local authorities who fail to provide accommodation for them.

Fears of house prices falling

The Crosscare Report also looked at the value of property in areas where Travellers sites were built. If the sites were there before settled people moved in there is no effect on property values. If Traveller sites were built later and were of a good standard and properly landscaped, again there was no identifiable effect on property values. "If sites are well maintained and kept small in size the impact is minimal" one estate agent reported.

There was one negative outcome in that sites built close to expensive housing estates, may initially have had an adverse effect on values. The report went on to say that this could easily be counteracted if Travellers were included in the planning, development and delivery of Traveller Accommodation.

The way forward

In 1986 the E.S.R.I. concluded in Report No. 131, "that the living conditions of Travelling People were intolerable". This analysis, at least as far as the 1200 families with no permanent home are concerned, is still true. The authors went on to say that "the problems were soluble given good and strong will. Remedies are at hand. They should be taken".

It seems to me, after my twelve years of involvement, that the "strong will" to resolve this matter is lacking in certain areas. We are now facing into a new millennium, a new era, and a new multicultural society. Is it too much to look for an intercultural approach to resolving issues? Are we going to go the road we have travelled so often in past decades; that of depending on new Equality and Equal Status Legislation and the Courts to give to Travellers a home of their own, appropriate to their culture and way of life?

In order to achieve what the E.S.R.I is suggesting then it seems imperative that Travellers and settled people will have to live side by side in a new multicultural society. At the moment separateness impacts far more on Travellers as it continues to ensure a real exclusion from Irish society. "No humane and decent society made aware of Travellers living conditions could permit them to persist". So concluded the *E.S.R.I. Report*.

Until the core conclusions of the CROSSCARE Report and the *The Report of the Task Force on the Travelling Community 1995* are acted upon, I remain to be convinced.

A prejudice exposed is a prejudice undermined

Cathleen McDonagh

The single most discriminated against ethnic group is the Travelling people

(European Report 1992)

Travellers in Irish settled society suffer from the experience of prejudice. From this prejudice comes an action which is termed "discrimination". Discrimination is the acting out of peoples' prejudice, which is not just a concept but a lived reality for Travellers. This reality is well documented by surveys. One such survey carried out by the Irish Traveller Movement quotes the following results

8 out of 10 Travellers refused in a pub
5 out of 10 Travellers asked to leave a shop
3 out of 10 Travellers asked to leave a hairdressers
2 out of 10 Travellers asked to leave a laundry
Almost all Travellers who have tried to book a hotel have experienced problems

There is no shortage of facts and reports confirming the reality of the discrimination that Travellers experience. Our second example confirms,

> Travellers are widely acknowledged as one of the most marginalised and disadvantaged groups in Irish society. Travellers fare poorly on every indicator used to measure disadvantage: unemployment, poverty, social exclusion, health status, infant mortality, life expectancy, illiteracy, formal education and training levels, access to decision making and political representation, gender equality, access to credit, accommodation and living conditions: it is not surprising, therefore, that the Economic and Social research Institute conclude "The circumstances of the Irish Travelling People are intolerable. No humane or decent society, once made aware of such circumstances, could permit them to persist" (Citizen Traveller 1999)

Discrimination – personal, interpersonal and institutional

The discrimination we experience can be termed "personal", "interpersonal" and "institutional". People treat us as objects when they refuse us services, such as refusing to allow us the use of hotels to hold functions, wedding receptions and social gatherings. When we are refused the use of a church to hold confirmations and when a group of teenage girls are refused entry into shops in Grafton Street, – being publicly humiliated by shop security and sales staff and escorted off Grafton Street for no reason other than that they were Travellers – these experiences of discrimination are termed "personal" and "interpersonal".

When procedures, practice and social policies are made in such a way that they do not take into account who we are as a people or reflect any awareness or acknowledgement of our culture, this is what is termed "institutional discrimination".

At the heart of all these forms of discrimination is a belief termed "ethnocentrism". This is a belief that one group of people's way of life is the best way to live and is the way every group should live, even if this way of life has to be forced on another group. Travellers in Ireland experience the effects of ethnocentrism. We, as a people suffer from discrimination as a result of the prejudice of the settled community towards the Traveller community. This experience of discrimination comes from a warped human reality that screams to be challenged and that has to be challenged, as it is an affront to the dignity of all humanity.

Although we use words like "personal", "interpersonal", and "institutional" to describe the different ways people experience discrimination, it can be hard to put a face on discrimination. For myself, the face I see is the pain on the face of the young person as they try to make sense of the rejection they have experienced; the eyes that hold back the tears of both anger and confusion as they speak of what has happened. It can be seen in the eyes of, the young person who cannot get into the disco, the middle- aged man trying to go for a social drink, the young family with nowhere to stay. The list can go on. I would ask the reader "What would you say to a child who asked you why?" "What would you say to the adult who tries to protect the young, knowing in their heart that they can't stop the experience of pain from happening time and time again to the child that they love?". It cuts like a knife into the heart and the wound stays open because it does not get the chance to heal. The one thing that Traveller parents know as they look at their child is, that though life holds enough troubles of its own, their loved child will have to enter into the bitter experience of discrimination no matter how hard they try to protect him/her. This is the legacy that prejudice passes on to our children as we enter into the year 2000. To truly challenge this experience we need to be aware of its root cause and in the case of discrimination this means uncovering and exploring the nature of prejudice.

The nature of prejudice

Prejudice, strictly defined, is a performed and unsubstantiated judgement or opinion about an individual or a group, either favourable or unfavourable in nature. In modern usage, however, the term most commonly denotes an unfavourable or hostile attitude towards other people based on their membership of another social or ethnic group. The distinguishing characteristic of a prejudice is that it is based on a stereotype (i.e. an oversimplified generalisation) about the group towards which the prejudice is directed.

(Microsoft Encarta 1993-1997)

Gordon W. Allport has suggested five stages of prejudice and several stages of acting out of prejudice. (i) Anti-locution which means hostile talk. (ii) Avoidance, (iii) Discrimination, (iv) Physical attacks (v) Extermination-genocide. (Allport, 1958.) The first three in this list are commonplace within the experience of anyone who is familiar with the reality of prejudice. Sadly in today's world as in the past we have ample evidence of all five stages being carried out. Kosovo is one of many examples of this in today's world. Another tragic example from the past is the treatment of the Jews, Gypsies and of others deemed as "outcasts of society" in Nazi death camps. It is a thin line that separates people going from stages one to three to the extreme of stages four and five.

Travellers make up less than 1% (0.6% in fact) of the population. We have suffered the experience of prejudice for too long. It has been carried onto each generation and it is getting worse. We as Travellers hear of the new problem of prejudice that has arisen in Ireland as a result of the arrival of refugees and asylum seekers in this country.

Prejudice is seen as a new concept in Irish society, but this is not so. What is a truer reading of the situation of prejudice in Ireland is that it is now coming to light as it comes out into the open. What we as Travellers have always experienced is now being given a more public face. We can take up the challenge that is there for us all, Traveller and settled alike, to create a society where all cultures can live side by side in equal respect of each other. This I believe is not an impossible dream; it is our true human reality that has been blinded by our fears and ignorance of our shared humanity. This suffering of people will continue until prejudice is challenged at its very core.

Racism

When we look to history we can see what happens to a society when its prejudiced beliefs are allowed to go unchecked. There is untold suffering for the victims of prejudice which is a poison that in the end destroys the very fabric of society. Prejudice blinds people to the diversity of human existence, which is seen to be a threat rather than an enrichment of society. It closes people's minds to the many cultural ways of existing within our shared world. Racism is an expression of this fear and ignorance towards people who are perceived to be a threat by others.

> Racism is a belief that cultural traits and capacities are racially determined. It justifies and acts upon the assumption that some races are naturally superior or inferior. The term racism is also applied to behaviour towards another race, which reflects these assumptions. Falsely ascribing inherited characteristics, personality and behaviour traits on a racial basis gives rise to prejudice, discrimination, scapegoating etc.
>
> (Pavee Point 1999)

At this time, we as a nation have yet to reach the "point of no return" when one will kill another in the form of ethnic cleansing, a sanitised term for the mass murder of a people deemed less than human, to satisfy our fears and prejudices as a society. There are two roads open to society. Which one will we take? The experience of Travellers in regards to prejudice confirms the road that we are taking at this time, a road that if we continue on, will only create more suffering and death. "Discrimination", "prejudice" and "racism" are terms that sum up an experience of pain shared by people who suffer from rejection which arises out of the ignorance of other people who fail to understand or accept the concepts of "Culture" or "Race".

Facing the challenge

What future do we create for our children? What lessons do we teach them in the present in regards to our humanity and our responsibility for what we create now and allow to be created in the future? At this time we have the power to choose. Do we choose to create for them a present and a future that give life or death?

Make no mistake, prejudice, discrimination and racism are very real and complex realities. There is an urgent need to understand what lies beneath the fears that give rise to them. The more we allow them to go unchecked and unchallenged the more we perpetuate the ignorance that forms the foundations of prejudice, discrimination and racism. There are vast accounts of research in the area of prejudice, and the more we research into these accounts the more we learn about the concepts that lie beneath them. By examining, for example, Nazi social theory we expose its myths on humanity and at the same time we can also discover the parallels that exist in all such warped beliefs of human understanding.[1]

Every prejudiced fear is a belief that has to be exposed, to be understood and challenged. It is only when we do this that we can work on the real fears and not the perceived ones, and in so doing we create a future that is one of hope for all.

The challenge is ours. If we do not face it, then the fruits of prejudice go unchecked and flourish. What will future generations say to this? What will we be held accountable for?

[1] The Irish Times Saturday, January 7th 1995 in an article titled *"Isolation reduces Travellers to social outcasts"* by Jim McLoughlin, we see that research into the concepts behind the Nazi beliefs gives some understanding of the workings of the Nazi social theory. This theory was and is based on a belief in the existence of a superior people struggling for space, what they considered to be their space taken over by others. The others in this case were not considered fully human. To the Nazis, their perceived struggle for existence meant a struggle for space. The article by Jim McLoughlin sees parallels between attacks on Travellers and Migrant workers in Europe, and the Nazi social theory.

My experience of discrimination

Winnie McDonagh

Discrimination, an all – pervasive reality

Prejudice and discrimination affect all areas of Traveller life and Travellers experience discrimination, which is almost a daily occurrence, in a variety of ways. Socialising is an area where Travellers experience discrimination in a very real way. I would love to be able to go out for a drink now and again with a few members of my family but the only times that I have gone out and have not had a problem is when there is only one or two of us together and, considering I have seven sisters and two brothers, this is not much of a family get-together! Discrimination is not just about being refused entry into pubs. I know and have seen how badly Travellers have been treated in supermarkets, hairdressers, libraries and shopping centres, in fact, almost everywhere Travellers have to avail of a service or facility. Sometimes if, as part of my work, I am organising a session or programme for the homework group on a particular issue or subject and I ask for help or for volunteers from a project or group in the settled community, most of the time settled people react very negatively.

One incident that I remember quiet well was when the Parish of the Travelling People was organising fund-raising for an orphanage in Romania. We had a group of young girls and boys in the after school group who wanted to do something for Fr. Dan who was organising the trip. One of the Traveller children suggested that they go up to the local Dunnes Stores (most of their mothers shop there) and pack bags to raise money. They had seen a local youth football club doing this and thought it was a good idea. The others, however, said that there was no point because they would not let Travellers in there. Fr. Dan and myself wrote a couple of letters of reference and sent them away to Dunnes Stores but we never got so much as a reply. The young people were very hurt by this and would say to me that they did not see any point in doing any of the things that Travellers are being told to do by settled people to improve themselves and their community. Why bother when they are going to have to come up against this type of thing? When you get incidents like this one, they set you back for a long time and then you have to start all over again re-building your confidence and self-esteem.

During my three years in Maynooth College studying youth and community work, I would often go out at night with other people on the course for a celebration meal or drink and there would be no problem. After I graduated, I went into a pub and ordered some food or drinks for some relations; there was no problem until later that evening when three of them arrived and were refused entry. The fact is that if they had known that I was a Traveller in the first place when I initially made arrangements with the staff, they would never have accommodated me.

Another area that is affected is the whole area of work, because while some Travellers may be happy enough to go out and look for a job it's not always that straightforward. We have had some young people who, rather than giving their real address which is the site, would have to use another place, such as a relative's house, to get a job. In my opinion, a growing number of Travellers would like jobs but it's not always possible for them to get one.

The nature of discrimination

Prejudice and discrimination are everywhere, it is almost as if as soon as you open your mouth and talk settled people realise what you are. Then a kind of a barrier comes down and people just won't accept or accommodate you. Sometimes you don't even recognise it for what it is, especially when it happens in small everyday situations. Some people may simply move away from you and sit on another chair, or they may pass a general comment about Travellers and then try to excuse themselves by saying that this comment does not refer to you. What they fail to realise is that if they discriminate against Travellers, they are discriminating against me, because they use words and phases such as "those people" "the Travellers"; they are referring to us all. The effects that such comments have are much greater than people often realise. It can knock the feet completely from under someone and the setbacks that it can cause are huge.

Sometimes people can use ignorance as their excuse by saying that they didn't know what they were doing. But there have been some situations where I have been present, and I could tell that the people responsible knew exactly what they were doing and they knew that it was unfair and that it wasn't right. It seems to give them some sense of power in being able to do this to another person and that's what I find totally unacceptable.

I like to think of myself as being fair-minded and I know that I have my own prejudices and can be discriminating myself, but I know that if I think and question or challenge myself, I can admit to my wrongdoing and apologise for it. There are people, however who just totally disregard the truth of their actions or who go along with what is the "flavour of the month". For instance all the recent racism has been directed towards the refugee or black people and it seems that all of a sudden the Travellers are not that bad after all, "It's all these foreigners". Yet if everyone was treated equally and fairly there would be no need for any one to be discriminated against.

The effects of discrimination

When I sit down and really think about the reality of discrimination, I have a great sense of disbelief at the whole unfairness of it. If you can see unfairness in a situation then it's logical to think that everyone else should be able to see it too.

What hurts and annoys me most, at times, is being in a group and seeing other people in my company who are hurt by something that is said or done, especially if they are in a place or premises for the very first time. I might brush it off because I know what society is like and I have experienced discrimination so many times in the past, but it doesn't make it any easier to watch others feeling embarrassed or hurt. You can distance yourself from the situation and, because of my training, I can say that I understand why some people act in that way; perhaps because they haven't been exposed to racism or to difference as I have been. Nevertheless, if you're there with two or three members of your family who don't understand and only see it for what it is then you can feel very hurt, even more so on their behalf than on your own.

If you have experienced discrimination for as long as Travellers have you get to the stage where you can't or don't challenge it. You would rather that the ground would open up and swallow you, so that you didn't have to look at the person who has offended you in the face. I have seen Travellers whom I would describe as being very strong and sure of themselves, actually clamming up completely when something like this happens to them. If there is a group of settled people looking on when a situation of discrimination arises, it can be difficult to react or even to ask for an explanation because, while you are trying to address the person who is being racist towards you, you are also conscious that the people on the outskirts are looking on. You also have a tendency to feel that the on-lookers presume that the Traveller has done something wrong. As one Traveller said to me,

> The other people looking know nothing about me. They don't know what type of person I am. But yet when they see me being turned away from a place they make an instant judgement that I am, or must be, an undesir-

able kind of person and I don't have or get a chance to explain myself or the situation. Even though I know that from what I have experienced, if I saw a settled person in need and being treated the same way, I would be very quick in standing up for them.

Our children – Traveller and settled – hope for the future?

Children are more accepting of each other than adults are. They see themselves firstly as children. When we, as adults, get involved in our children's lives, in addition to passing on the good things we also pass on all our prejudices and negative opinions, and all of these influence our children, in good and bad ways. Perhaps we do it with the best of intentions, but sometimes we impose our ideas, our beliefs and how we see people, onto our children. This happens in both the Traveller and settled communities. I don't think there's an easy solution to this but what I try to do is to point out to my children that life, whether you're a Traveller or a settled person, is not easy or perfect. Although I may want my children to have some contacts or relationships with settled people, that's not to say that I want them to experience all that is negative in that community as well or that I want them to become like settled people. Initially people growing up see themselves only as children, but when they come to a certain age they begin to see themselves in terms of their backgrounds, family etc. and become very aware of themselves as either Travellers or settled people.

When my eldest daughter is in school or joins some of her classmates on trips or social events, or goes away with them as part of a group, she would be very confident in herself as a Traveller. She is very much aware that in whatever she is doing that she should not deny or lose her identity and that she does not have to become different than what she is in order to participate with settled people. Of course there are limits and boundaries around certain issues and behaviour that she is aware of. The group of friends that she has accept her as a Traveller, they haven't tried to change her and would be very open to hearing her views and opinions. I feel that she is sensible and knows about the dangers out there and how to keep herself safe. I know that the settled people that she is with, are a group of genuine young people, and whether your child's friends are Travellers or settled is unimportant, as long as she or he is in good company.

Sometimes members of the Traveller community will look at the settled community and only see the drug-addiction and the sleeping around, and that's why they don't want their children mixing with settled people, because they are afraid of what their children may become involved in. I am not saying that young Travellers are totally isolated or protected from reality, but parents tend to very protective of their children and are very aware of peer pressure. I think that in some ways Traveller parents feel that if their children don't have contact with members of the settled community, then hopefully certain issues or dangers, such as drug-addiction, will go away and won't ever have to be dealt with.

Some concluding thoughts – celebrating difference

I would hope that settled people would be more accepting, more open-minded and maybe be more willing to sit down and listen to Travellers rather than making assumptions about them or making judgements, either automatically or on very little information. At times I find in talking to settled people that I am constantly being taken apart and looked at in bits and pieces and then, being put back together. If I don't meet or fit settled people's expectations or assumptions of what I am or how I should be, then it appears that there's something fundamentally wrong with me and therefore, I am completely disregarded. I hope that people wouldn't be frightened of Travellers or frightened of becoming involved with Travellers. If you are open and accepting then you can accept people as people with all their frailties.

If I didn't know anything at all about the settled community, I could choose only to see settled people in negative terms, as drug-takers or as people who are involved in under-age drinking and who let their young people roam around the streets at all hours of the day and night. If I only saw settled people in that light it wouldn't be a true picture. I think you have to realise that everything is not just black and white. There are many sides to everything and you have to be willing to learn about people. If you are willing to sit down and accept people and learn from them, then you are half-way there.

I get great enjoyment when I meet a group of ethnic women at the various seminars and meetings that I go to, where there may be one or two other Travellers, a Jewish woman or women from Jamaica, South Africa, China or somewhere else. It's great to sit down and compare different people's cultures, lives, traditions and customs in a positive rather than in a negative way. Why do we always seem to get caught up in the negative differences and why can't we see what's behind the type of dress or costume people wear and the traditions and customs they follow? I think once you get beyond that and see people as people, then you can learn a lot of things from them.

Primary Health Care for Travellers project

Pavee Point Women

> From birth to old age those at the bottom of the scale have much poorer health and quality of life than those at the top. Gender, area of residence and ethnic origin also have a deep impact.
>
> *The Black Report, U.K. 1980*

Context

The health of Travellers is greatly influenced by various other aspects of their lives which include the stress and loss of self-esteem generated by living in a hostile society where discrimination and racism are daily facts of life. Traveller children grow up witnessing evictions, harassment, institutionalised segregation at school and in the welfare system, being refused service on the basis of their ethnic identity, and being made to feel very much marginalised. These experiences create enormous personal stress and anxiety and adversely affect health and self – esteem.

Studies of Native American Indians and Australian Aboriginals as well as of immigrant ethnic minorities in Britain show that high rates of accidental death, alcoholism, violence (especially against women), chaotic personal and family lives, glue sniffing and drug addiction have all been associated with the effects of living in a racist society . Some of these problems which indicate serious cultural stress are present among Irish Travellers. Many of these types of health problems are not amenable to simple personal health service solutions. Another stress - inducing factor in Travellers' lives are the various obstacles (especially in terms of acquiring good quality accommodation) that have been put in place by governments and local authorities.

Traveller health – some special considerations

Travellers require special consideration in health care because they are a distinct cultural group with different perceptions of health, disease and care needs. The Health Status Study in 1987 has shown that Travellers have different health and disease problems to settled people. This study showed a large divide between Traveller health and settled people's health. It highlighted the fact that Travellers only now reach the life expectancy of the settled population in the nineteen forties and that the infant mortality in the Traveller population was three times the national average. Life expectancy was 12 years less for Traveller women and 10 years less for Traveller men as compared to the settled community.

Factors which impact on Travellers health

There are a number of issues that affect Travellers' health including accommodation, discrimination and lack of awareness of services and the barriers to access of services.

Accommodation

Traveller sites are often located beside dumps with noxious fumes and vermin; graveyards or main roads with a higher risk of accidental injury. Currently approximately 1,200 families live on the side of the road with no access to water, toilets, and electricity or refuse collection. Many sites are located a long way from health centres, are not serviced by public transport and do not have a postal service.

> Some postmen do not deliver post to unofficial sites, and some only go to official sites, when they have a bag full of post, this means that sometimes we miss our appointments or we get them too late and then hospitals are complaining that Travellers never turn up for their clinics.
> Mary Collins Community Health worker, *PHC for Travellers Project.*

Poor living conditions mean that Travellers suffer from more diseases and illness and are less likely to look after their health as they have difficulty preparing for and attending hospital or doctor appointments due to lack of facilities and childcare responsibilities.

> Hospitals often give Travellers clinic appointments for 9am in the morning, this is very difficult if you live on an unofficial site and you have no facilities like running water, there is no buses and you have no time to get ready, as it takes you all you can do to get the children ready for school on time.
> Tessa Collins Community Health worker, *PHC for Travellers Project.*

Discrimination

Ireland like many other countries has always tried to portray an image of itself as a country where racism and discrimination don't exist, but this is not the reality for Travellers. Discrimination affects many aspects of Traveller life, attending school, shopping, going to the doctor, to hospitals, to pubs, to cinemas, or even just getting a taxi. Travellers are followed around shops, doctors won't enrol them, and they are segregated in school. They will not be allowed into pubs and cinemas will often refuse them. This discrimination causes much mental stress and has a negative effect on Travellers' health.

> A lot of doctors refuse to take Travellers on their list, this means you have no way of getting treatment for your family when they are sick and you have to wait until the health board force a doctor to take you on and this can take months.
> Lena Lawrence Community Health worker, *PHC for Travellers Project.*

The Primary Health Care for Travellers Project

In October 1994 *the Primary Health Care for Travellers Project* began in the Finglas/Dunsink areas of Community Care Area 6 (CCA6) in the Eastern Health Board. The project is a partnership between Pavee Point and the Eastern Health Board.

The Overall Aim of the project is:

To improve the health status and quality of life of the Traveller community in that area (CCA6).

The four objectives of the project are to:

♦ Establish a model of Traveller participation in the promotion of health.

♦ Develop the skills of Traveller women in providing community based services

♦ Liase and assist in creating dialogue between Travellers and health service - providers in the area

♦ Highlight gaps in the Health Service delivery to Travellers in Community Care Area 6 and work towards reducing inequalities that exist in established services.

Current position

The Primary Health Care for Travellers project has been established seven years ago. It was the first health care project to be undertaken by Travellers for Travellers. It now has sixteen trained Traveller community health workers who are employed by Pavee Point with funding provided by the Eastern Health Board. In 1999 it extended its working area into the Blanchardstown sites, so that it is now working with approximately two-hundred and seventy Traveller families.

Baseline Survey of Health Problems and Needs of Travellers

We, as Traveller community health workers, carried out a baseline survey in 1995 with eighty-eight Traveller families living in five sites in Community Care Area 6 to identify the health needs of Travellers. (i.e. to give a baseline of disease pattern and utilisation of service at the time before starting the programme). We were trained to design a questionnaire and we went out and asked Traveller women questions.

We then organised a workshop with the Travellers from the community to feedback the results. We then got information from health service providers and met with them to discuss issues emerging. A joint session was then organised for Travellers together with health providers to agree the areas of most need, which were identified as the following: women's health, nutrition, dental health, child health and environmental health.

The following are some of our results:

One of the most interesting findings was the huge information gap that existed in regard to health (fig. 1) Travellers did not know why, where, how or and when to access health services.

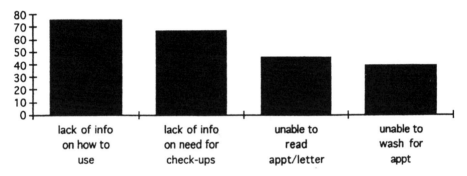

Fig. 1 Reasons given for not understanding entitlements within health services

The most common reason given for not understanding entitlements within the health services was a lack of information on how to use services (this reason was given by 76 women i.e. 97% of the respondents).

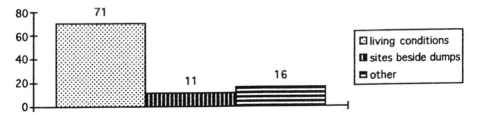

Fig. 2 Why Travellers have more illness than others.

Eighty-four respondents (95%) said that they thought Travellers had more illnesses than settled people. The reason for this was, they thought, very clear; the living conditions (bad accommodation) (fig. 2). Given that this was an open-ended question and no possible answers were suggested, the overwhelming response indicates that living conditions was the cause of Travellers having more illness than others.

use healers 81% **don't use healers 19%**

Fig. 3 Number who attend a healer when sick.

The vast majority of families (81%) said that they used healers. This is an important finding given the proposed intervention by Community Health Workers. The tendency for Travellers to seek cures is already known.

In figure 4 the illnesses for which they do so are shown

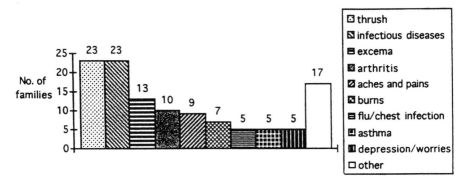

Fig 4 Illnesses for which cures are sought.

Cures are most commonly sought for thrush or infectious diseases.

The respondents were asked to suggest changes to the health services, which they thought, would be useful. A total of 123 suggestions were given and of these 54 women (44%) suggested more culturally-appropriate information to be available to Travellers. (Fig. 5)

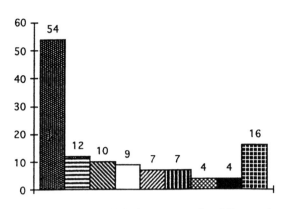

Fig. 5 Useful changes to health services.

Ongoing work of the Primary Health Care Project

Child Health

We work with the public health nurse on the sites to increase Traveller women's knowledge about the importance of child development and immunisation clinics. Many of the Traveller children have ear problems and so we go with them to Sr. Lydia's clinic in Cabra and also to Temple Street Hospital for Ear, Nose and Throat Clinics where children get grommets fitted to help prevent deafness.

Kathleen Joyce, Community Health worker, *PHC for Travellers Project.*

Women's Health

We made an arrangement with the Well Woman clinic so that we could block book clinics with them. We go onto the sites and explain to other Traveller women why they should look after themselves and go for screening, then we arrange a clinic and go with them for cervical smears, breast examinations and family planning advice. We do this on a regular basis.

At the start of the project women were very nervous as they had never been for smear tests, and they were uncomfortable about discussing these issues, but now they come looking for us to make appointments. Since the project started many women have been found who had problems but have now received treatment.

Nancy McDonnell, Community Health worker, *PHC for Travellers Project*.

Dental health

A dental initiative was also started, with special clinics being held in Ballygall and Roselawn Health Centres in the evening to facilitate access for all the family. We have also organised on-site dental screening at St. Joseph's site in Finglas.

Nutrition

A nutrition programme was developed with the community nutritionist from the EHB, and we will commence work on this out on the sites in early 2000.

Health education materials

We have also been involved in the design of Health Education posters on Breast Feeding, Immunisation, Burns, Healthy Eating and Dental Health. A video on Traveller women's health has also been produced which will be launched in early 2000. We are also hoping to produce a Traveller Child Health video in 2000. These Health Education materials reflect Traveller Culture and feature Travellers in them and so are more meaningful and more easily understood by Travellers.

Through the programme greater awareness has been created about the needs, entitlements and possibilities in the health services, as well as the difficulties of accessing services that should be available.

In-service training

The primary health care project had also provided in-service training to a range of health professionals. We hope that through this work we will encourage health personnel to offer a more culturally-appropriate service and to work towards an increase in the utilisation of essential services.

This is the first time Travellers have got this type of training and job. We understand our own people and believe that given the proper support and resources we can begin to improve the health of our community. It is no longer acceptable that Travellers die young.

Missie Collins, Community Health worker, *PHC for Travellers Project.*

Areas of progress at a national policy level

Since 1994 a number of important policy documents have been produced which have had huge implications for Traveller Health. Some of these developments are as follows:

The National Traveller Health Advisory committee

The National Travellers Health Advisory Committee was established in November 1998. It is made up of representatives of, various divisions in the Department of Health, the Health Boards and national Traveller organisations. Its brief includes the following:

◆ drawing up a national policy for a health strategy to improve the health statues of the Traveller community.

◆ ensuring that Traveller health is a priority area within the Department of Health and setting targets against which performance can be measured;

◆ ensuring co-ordination, collection and collation of data on Travellers' health;

◆ supporting health boards in developing strategies to improve Traveller access to health services;

◆ providing a forum for the discussion of health initiatives for Travellers and for ongoing consultation with Travellers and Traveller organisations on health service delivery to Travellers.

Since the NTHAC was established it has focused its attention on the development of a National Traveller Health Strategy which should be available by March 2000. This document will inform the future direction in Travellers' health and well as providing direction for the regional Traveller Health Units.

Traveller Health Units

Each health board should have a committee drawn from the various sectors in the health board and from local Travellers and Traveller organisations. They have a reporting relationship to each of the

Programme Managers. These Units should incorporate existing inter-sectoral structures focusing on Traveller Health issues at health board level. The brief suggested for these units includes the following:

♦ monitoring the delivery of health services to Travellers and set-ting regional targets against which performance can be measured;

♦ ensuring that Traveller health is given prominence on the agenda of the health board;

♦ ensuring co-ordination and liaison within the health board, and between the health board and other statutory and voluntary bod-ies, in relation to the health situation of Travellers;

♦ collection of data on Traveller health and utilisation of health ser-vices;

♦ ensuring appropriate training of health service providers in terms of their understanding of and relationship with Travellers.

♦ supporting the development of Traveller specific services, either directly by the health board or, indirectly through funding appro-priate voluntary organisations.

Resources

In 1998 for the first time the Department of Health released addi-tional resources specifically for Travellers' Health. In the first year, £0.5 million was provided to enable the establishment of Traveller Health Units by all Health Board and to initiate some projects in rela-tion to Travellers' health. £0.9 million was provided by the Department in 1999 and the plan is to double this budget in the year 2000. These monies have been distributed to the health boards depending on the population of Travellers in their area. This has facil-itated the development of new initiatives for Travellers e.g. seven areas around the country are now replicating the PHC for Travellers project.

These are promising new developments, but unfortunately it will take time for these new developments to impact on Travellers' health status on the ground. To date only six of the eight health boards have set up a Traveller Health Unit and some of those established have not followed the guidelines in *the Task Force report*.

Our hope for the new millennium is to see improvements in the health status of Travellers and in their treatment in society.

Appendix One

Shift in National Policy context

National Health Strategy – May 1994
Developing a Policy for Women's Health – June 1995
Task Force on the Travelling community – July 1995
Plan for Women's Health – April 1997

These policies have implications for Travellers' health. The following are some of the highlights in the policies, which apply directly to Travellers' Health.

◆ The success of the *Primary Health Care for Travellers Project* and its endorsement as a national model.

◆ The change in policy context, which recognises Traveller culture, and the specific health needs of Travellers.

◆ Acknowledgement of the need for new structures to facilitate the participation of Travellers.

◆ The recognition of the importance of working in partnership with the voluntary sector.

◆ Release of additional resources for the development of initiatives for Travellers in Health.

◆ Acknowledgment of the impact of accommodation on the health status of Travellers.

New structures

These new structures are very welcome and are to be set up in accordance with the recommendations outlined in the Health Chapter in the *Report of Task Force on the Travelling Community 1995*. These new structures have a commitment to the inclusion of Travellers and Traveller organisations and form the basis of a partnership approach to working towards an improvement in Travellers' Health.

Travellers, minorities, and schools

Máirín Kenny

The challenge of cultural diversity

The arrival of 'Y2K' is a good moment to review how services for Travellers have developed. Taking formal education provision, I will focus on, how teachers' roles have developed, and on our teacher training, particularly in relation to how social exclusion is read and addressed in the formal school system. Because it's not so much what we see as the way that we see it, that informs what we do. Thirty years ago we were at best struggling with the idea of there being such a thing as a marginalised, let alone a cultural minority in Ireland.

As the First Commission Report notes, the plight of Travellers 'has not troubled the public conscience to any degree' (*The Report of the Commission on Itinerancy 1963*). Well warranted intervention began but Travellers were presumed to be a disadvantaged group whose marginalisation would vanish when the doors to life chances accessible to the majority were open to them also. Then in the 1980s new thinking challenged the perception of Travellers that informed intervention (O'Connell, 1992) and the debate over their ethnic identity gathered real force. In the school arena, pressure from Travellers and their teachers is gradually gaining recognition for Traveller culture. Yet our society is increasingly intent on controlling diversity, an urge forcefully expressed in our continued exclusion of Travellers and in our noisy noxious attempts to close our doors to immigrants. As educators we must counter this hardening of the attitudes, with a rattling of the categories.

The role of education

Exploration of identies lies at the core of education and all of us gain from exploring questions of identity – who am I/are we/you/they?. The richer, the more open, flexible and happily unfinished our responses to these questions, the better educated we are (Kenny, 1997). Nothing focuses the mind like the law; with the new *Education Act (1998)*, issues relating to legal rights to inclusion in mainstream have a new urgency.

Teachers, as agents of change in responding to new challenges

In dealing with the presence of Traveller pupils, schools encountered issues relating to diversity, ethnicity and racism that scarcely got nodding recognition in teacher training, curricula, textbooks, or – crucially - research. Our education system was slow off the mark. Reiss's (1975) study of Traveller education in England is a product of a system whose investment in research was well ahead of ours, maybe because the presence of many other minorities had forced some degree of critical analysis on the English system. We ploughed on, innocent of research or theoretical debate; perhaps because, as we are often told, Irish teachers are so intelligent and creative, in parts we made a fair job of reinventing the wheel. But canonising pragmatism at the expense of analysis is indicative of a great waste of resources on both fronts.

Teachers can be critical and proud of their role in the development that occurred. Some early blunders are obvious, like the special classes with washing facilities that schools wouldn't be caught dead with today. But we also sailed into territory proper to other professionals; early ATTP (Association of Teachers of Travelling People) newsletters abound with statements on family stability, alcoholism, housing. Issues like inadequate insecure accommodation severely constrain what can be done in school, and many teachers expended huge energy trying to address them, and to support families living under terrible stress in dire conditions. Did some in the process slip into becoming amateur social workers; and did the traumas we witnessed traumatise us, so that we didn't demand as much as we might have from the children? Some of the adult Travellers who now say they weren't pushed enough, came to school from those dire conditions. And the ITM's Report on Travellers and post primary education (1997) quotes Travellers who say that some teachers still demand too little of their children. By getting involved in broader, and arguably more fundamental issues of community justice teachers can help to lay the foundations necessary to the progress of children in school but such involvement can come to take priority over the teacher's primary responsibility which is ensuring that the children do the best they can in school. It's a see-saw but any professional's first duty to the cause of justice is, so to speak, to 'look after the day job' and to give all the energy needed to doing a good professional job.

The need for new, up-to-date teacher-training

Teachers of Travellers, like perhaps any of their colleagues in separate special provision, tended to be marginalised with their pupils. Working outside a mainstream context encourages starting from scratch, devising curricula, materials, tests, etc. – which may well have already been brought to a level of sophistication in research and practice relating to children from comparable groups. Perhaps this segregation explains the non-protest at the contrast between the level of investment in research and evaluation in, for instance, Van Leer projects for inner city children, and the almost total non-investment in research and evaluation in educational interventions for Travellers. Expenditure on provision for Travellers has been high but practice has progressed mainly through on-the-ground ad hoc inspiration. We shouldn't rest with that. Classroom teachers, the majority sector of the profession, will continue to be the key deliverers of formal schooling so they must have training opportunities to develop the skills and insights crucial to ensuring quality. The increasing range of specialist teachers also need training appropriate to their roles, whether that be remedial teaching, counselling, home-school liaison or adult education. And good teamwork demands clear, constantly reviewed and renewed statements of the roles of each sector, a task in which all the stakeholders in the school system should be involved.

High quality intercultural teacher – training

What is the purpose of this call for new training; or, to put it another way, which children's needs generate the call? Traveller pupils awoke many teachers to the value of ethnic diversity, and now schools must welcome greater and richer variety as other minorities arrive. The inclusion of children with disabilities in mainstream education further challenged the standardising thrust of the system. The response of mainstream children in classroom and playground exemplifies the ignorance of the dominant majority, the maintainers and beneficiaries of marginalising practices. So, all children need, to be schooled in inclusive thinking and practice, to learn that the majority ethnic culture is not 'normal' or inherently superior, and to learn to respect and welcome individual and group diversity. Otherwise, access to mainstream remains just that: minorities are physically present but their distinctive identities, strengths and needs are not registered. But efforts to meet new and newly recognised needs cannot be allowed to somehow ride piggy-back on existing training which barely addressed the issues involved, if at all. In relation to ethnicity, there must be adequate investment in high quality intercultural anti-racism training. This should be solidly based on good classroom practice, substantially designed and delivered by good classroom practitioners. Let us fight every onset of piggy-backing, all slippage towards amateurism which can only de-professionalise and disempower service deliverers. That is essential if we are to ensure that mainstream provision and specialist supports are truly empowering, truly educational for the whole community.

Analysis of structural discrimination as key to finding new and effective educational responses

You could say the system breaks across teachers' backs: they mediate interaction between school provision on one side, and parents and children on the other. From my analysis of interviews with many teachers of Travellers, I will give a few indicators of how the system works through them. They talked, often very positively, about Traveller culture and, often very angrily, about the structural discrimination their pupils endured. But when I asked what blocked progress in the classroom, they applied the kind of causal analysis we all learned in college. Pupils' problems were seen as rooted in their emotional instability, low self-image and fear of challenge, and these were traced to family factors. And the teachers were deeply demoralised by their own failure to address this pain adequately. Their analysis and responses were examples of 'mothering discourse' (Acker, 1995) which typically is punishingly high on teacher commitment, but low on political analysis. With different training, that included study of how structural factors affect pupil performance, these teachers could have interlinked personal/familial problems with oppressive social structures – both of which they identified clearly. Such contextual interpretations can suggest new responses. It also illuminates the limits of what teachers can achieve in any school, however inclusive, nested as all schools are in a racist society.

This fracture pervades much of our pedagogy. For instance, many personal growth and self-esteem programmes focus on the personal and interpersonal and bypass the structural. But it isn't true that all you need is to believe enough in yourself and you can do anything. The evidence indicates that to be, for instance, President of the US, you must be white, male and rich. Pupils need to learn to engage in honest, age-appropriate ways with the reality of structural injustices and how to confront them. A first analytical step, it seems to me, is to locate the cause of the ethnic minority child's pain in racism. Children's reactions to racism are similar to the reactions of children who are targets of any of many other forms of exclusion. Outcomes of exclusion are only partly addressed by self-esteem work, even in the context of acceptance and success in an inclusive school environment. Some children need more than that.

Anti-Racist awareness – essential to teacher – training

Teachers have not been adequately trained to cope with the effects of and indeed the continuation of racism and other forms of exclusion-ary practice in schools. However, Bagley (1992) found that many teachers rejected the idea that they needed anti-racism training: they argued that as professionals they treated all children equally. But let us consider, did we female teachers see the sexism in how schools treated us as children? Did we oppose or continue it in our teaching? The sad answer is, we suffered it and then we passed it on in our deal-ings with female pupils, and it took us a long time to recognise both facts. If we were (and often still are) numbed to a discriminatory sys-tem that damaged ourselves, how can we claim full alertness to our probable collusions with systems that benefit us as white, or middle class, or settled, or highly educated, or able-bodied people? But many teachers in Bagley's study dismissed the idea that children's play-ground name-calling for instance could be racist. They argued that it was just children, that a child who happened to be fat, pimply, etc., would run that gauntlet too. I suggest that none of this labelling is interpersonal: the labelling denotes a categorisation process that marks the initiation of discrimination. A non-standard feature is fixed on by the 'normal' (= dominant) group as a category marker which will serve to justify excluding the mark carrier. It is child X as a 'fatty' or whatever, not child X as an individual, who is jeered. Thus it can all start: the target person, marked by ethnic status, colour, gender, sex-ual orientation, disability, features, etc. is reduced to being a repre-sentative of a rejected category. Can children act thus? (Short and Carrington 1992) argue that the child-centred ideology informing teacher training is naïve in teaching that though children can behave anti-socially they are free from malicious intent; and that they aren't 'ready' for abstract 'political' concepts until late in childhood. They can't understand racism, so a child's hostility towards a minority child cannot be read as racist. But the evidence is that they do understand, even at age three, what they are doing when they jeer or exclude a minority classmate. And clearly, if they can operate the notions they can discuss them in an age-appropriate way. But they won't do this if the teacher reads their behaviour simplistically and lets the system, in the person of the little bullies, off the hook.

The school's compliance in reproducing structures of exclusion

But children only follow the example of society and its schools who have been and are, guilty of deeming a person or group to be entirely defined by the category marker – so 'the blind' were all directed to work in telephony for instance; or Travellers were all deemed to be always and ever deprived in every sense of the term. Some categories are made up of individual members linked by nothing more than their 'target' trait; others have or develop group identities, sharing religious beliefs, social practices - culture. Travellers' experience suggests that groups kept fragmented by dominant social pressure may well have more difficulty having their ever changing, subtle and often non-material culture seriously recognised. Nonetheless if a society is intent on marginalising a group, the absence of noticeable markers can be read as proof of the group's deviance: the non-visibility of Jews in pre-war Germany was taken as proof of their deviously hidden difference, and they were made wear stars to 'out' them (Miles, 1993). To return to the school domain: precisely because the experience of marginal categories and groups is silenced, schools can miss the point: that structures of exclusion are being reproduced in what looks like 'just children fighting'. It goes on under our noses.

Blinded by custom and habit, we underestimate the gravity of the crime of exclusion. A summary of (Melzak's 1995) observations regarding refugee children is useful. She finds that not all who experience violence are traumatised, but those who are, need help to recover their resilience. The most therapeutic thing for them is finding a place in the community and school, and their difficulties in finding this highlight inadequacies in our society and school system.

Professionals know, from work and personal experience, the emotions on the continuum leading to trauma - loss, sorrow, anxiety, denial, insecurity, delusion, overreactions, fear that speaking about experience will affect loved ones; difficulty in building new relationships. However, we tend to pass on too quickly, for instance not making allowances for delayed reactions, over-confident that new experience will heal the child.

These observations could have been made about how some Traveller children, or indeed children from any marginal minority, respond to oppression. So there are useful common threads but each group requires opportunities appropriate to itself if it is to reclaim its space in the sun. For instance, in *The Report on Travellers and Refugees in Tallaght* (McVeigh & Binchy, 1998), a woman is quoted speaking of her descent into hopelessness as she waits and waits for word as to whether or not she can stay. The speaker could have been a Traveller or refugee, but the right response for one could well be wrong for the other.

Equality in education

To treat everyone equally is not to give everyone the same but to suit each one equally well. In schools, to 'treat all children the same' means to reflect the full variety of the wider community's experience as normal in the school environs and in the intercultural anti-racist curricula and materials, and to expect all pupils to reach their full potential. And while accentuating the positive, the school must avoid anaesthetising itself again to the depth of the injuries our society continues inflicting through racism and all forms of discrimination. So as in relation to any area in which equity is under threat, schools must adopt and implement a policy on anti-racism and interculturalism. Right of access, crucial though it is, is only stage one: children must not find their life experience, positive and negative, drowned out of the discourse of normality in the school. If their story isn't there, neither are they in the real sense of the term and the silenced child is under enormous pressure to become like everyone else in order to belong. So variety is killed.

The way forward

To that tired, cross old question, 'but what do Travellers want?', one could answer: like all of us, Travellers want normality - normal access to the normal services, schooling included. But to succeed, even in a welcoming school, some minority children and families need the support of psychological and social services, etc. Equity demands that schools honestly identify and assert those needs, and seek the supports to address them so that each and all pupils are called on to produce what should be their normal performance - their best one. Teachers need training to walk many razors' edges - to address symptoms of trauma appropriately in school while holding fast to the purpose of schooling; to register and respond in sound educational terms both to what is common and to what is distinctive across the various forms of discrimination and their outcomes. Finally: diverse practices of discrimination are informed by similar deep dynamics, and the dominant majority maintain them; therefore, children from this sector have most need to learn to recognise these practices, then drop them and try to stop them. We all must remember that to brush any group or person aside, to collude with any oppression, is to open the door to all forms of discrimination.

A Traveller woman's perspective on education

Winnie McDonagh

Traveller education project – providing support to Traveller families

I work as Education Development Worker with Traveller Education Support Options Project (T.E.S.O.), which is a Traveller education project based in Finglas. My work is part-time i.e. three and a half days a week, and involves liasing with and supporting families, children and local schools. The work also involves organising and setting up support structures such as homework groups, reading groups, after-school activities etc. These supports are for the children on the site and in the Finglas area. We in T.E.S.O, work from an office, which is based on the site. We support parents by holding meetings where they can discuss relevant issues and by facilitating meetings between parents and school principals or teachers. We also offer in-service training for the staff in the school in regard to Traveller culture, lifestyle etc. Basically, working on this project is about ensuring that support is there for families, children and schools in a variety of different ways.

Formal education/schooling

I value education for myself and for my children and I believe that it's going to play a big part in Travellers' lives more so in the future. Already, I can see this happening in the number of women who are on different courses at present. In the past most Traveller women went on courses where they could get training and an allowance or payment and these courses more often than not involved self-esteem and confidence building, and challenged women to look at themselves as individuals and at their place in their community. Now some of these women have moved onto other courses and Traveller women are realising more and more that if you want to move onto another course or a better one these days, you need to be able to read and write fairly well. You cannot stay at the same place or at the same level forever.

That's not to say however that all Travellers are interested or see a huge value in academic learning. Most of them would be more interested in learning practical things that would help them to make a living. So when I talk about education I wouldn't limit it to just either formal education or informal, or academic versus practical. I would say it's up to individuals themselves to know and to be encouraged, to find out where their strengths and weaknesses are and to pursue their area of interest. While I don't think that education is, or should be, about starting at pre-school level and ending at university, nevertheless, you still need basic reading and writing skills.

Each and every person is entitled to and should get a good basic education because education is a life-long process. I think for people like Travellers and others it's something they can leave and come back into at different stages in their lives, but you need to have a good level of reading and writing to be able to do that.

I wouldn't have had a proper or formal education myself. I left school early not having attended very regularly but because I am a good reader and writer I can and have gone back and done courses at third level or other courses that would be on offer or that are of interest to me or my work.

Parental views on the value of formal education

I think if you're talking to Traveller parents about education for Travellers or Traveller children, there is still a lot of confusion about the role that they think education plays in the lives of Travellers. Most would see the ability to read and write as sufficient. On the one hand for instance some of the women who are on training courses see it as necessary to them in order for them to participate in a course or to get work. On the other hand these same women may see ongoing formal education as not being of value in their children's lives, because the whole idea of going to school, from pre-school, right through to third level is not at the forefront of Travellers' minds.

Some Travellers (very small numbers) are coming around to regard formal education as something they want for their children, because they want to see them benefiting from education even though sometimes the benefits don't come as quickly as they may want them to. The rewards are not immediate whereas if you're on a training course an immediate reward is there.

We've had some young people in the our area leaving schools or courses so as to have a wage at the end of the week. They're dropping out of school for that reason, but that is happening in the settled community too. In saying that, however, the project on which I'm working has only been in operation for the last three years and in that time we have gone from having almost no-one in secondary school to having a group of seven to eight attending three local secondary schools. Some are preparing for their Junior and Leaving Certificates. We're delighted that they are getting to that level but we don't see anything happening beyond that point at this moment in time. At present, the numbers are only small, but hopefully, this will change in time. I would hope to see, in time, some of the young people staying on until Leaving Certificate and further.

Barriers to education

• The lack of necessity of education

There are many background factors and barriers, (social, economic, family, traditions etc.) that will determine whether or not Traveller children actually continue on in school to Leaving Certificate and beyond. In addition to this, Travellers themselves see other concerns as being of more value to their lives than education which is far from what they see as being vital or necessary. There is however a growing awareness about the need for education and certainly Travellers do regard basic reading and writing skills as necessary. What follows depends on the individual or family circumstances.

• Parents' negative experience of education

Another reason why Traveller parents are reluctant to send their children to school is their own experience of schooling. If they've had a good and positive experience themselves, as some Travellers have had, they feel happy about sending their children to school. If however I'm talking to parents who've gone through what used to be a "special class" system and who have had a segregated-type education or have experienced discrimination within the class and school, they will be less inclined to regard education as being very important for their children. When they reflect on their own hurtful or discomforting experience, they don't want their child or children going through a similar experience. They can be very protective of their children. They might say for example " My child is not going to school to be taken out for a shower" or "My child is not going to be talked about in the schoolyard, or be left with a group of Travellers all by themselves." Or, (as was told to me) "My child is not going to be taken on a school trip with a group of handicapped children only, like I was myself," because being a Traveller to some people means being mentally deficient in some way.

• Threat to cultural identity

There is also a fear among some Travellers that formal education educates Traveller children "out of" their own culture. In some ways formal education is seen to work contrary to, rather than in harmony with, Traveller values and culture. The fact that the curriculum is so monocultural and fails to recognise Traveller culture means that Travellers can feel isolated in school and learning can be seen as irrelevant because it does not address their experience. This leads to a type of shying away from, and scepticism towards, education.

When you look at and hear all of this experience you begin to understand the fears and concerns of Travellers. You can only try and encourage them by making it clear that you understand and respect their experience, but that hopefully things are changing within the schools for the better.

My children's experience of education

I have two daughters. The eldest is coming to the end of secondary school. She is doing her Leaving Certificate this year and the youngest has just gone into secondary school. The eldest girl has been in mainstream classes since she started school and she has had little or no outright experience of discrimination through primary school or secondary school. This is perhaps due to the fact that she was the only Traveller in the school or class and people didn't know or realise that she was a Traveller. She was accepted as a person before people realised she was a Traveller and while she believes that this has helped her, she feels that it should not have to be like this.

The youngest has just gone into first year. In her school there are a small group of Traveller girls from the halting site and Traveller houses. These are relations and friends. She is very much a Traveller, she wears the big earrings and uses certain words and the kind of expressions that Travellers use and she also goes to school with this group of girls. In this way, she is more openly identified as being a Traveller.

Some of her friends and cousins have parents whose experience of education may have been very negative and so their expectations of their children continuing on in school are limited somewhat and they may be more concerned with them making a good marriage or getting jobs. She is at times influenced by this way of thinking or talking.

She's not, so far, as focused on education as her sister is who from an early age wanted to go to secondary school and, hopefully, to go to college. My oldest daughter is very sure about the kind of work she wants to do and what she needs in terms of qualifications to do this work. On the other hand, like the rest of her friends, the youngest girl is at present more interested in clothes, fashion, getting a job, getting married etc., and school and a career are not on her mind. In saying that, they're two individuals. The youngest was always a mixer, while the eldest kept mostly to herself and so studying is easier for her. She'll sit there for hours with books reading, whereas the youngest comes in from school, throws down her school bag, saying she'll do her homework later on and asks if she can go out with her friends.

People think that Travellers don't work or they're all on social welfare. That's not necessarily true either but you have to take into account the discrimination and prejudice that is out there. This can have huge effects on people like Travellers who have to cope with it everyday of their lives. My two sons are fortunate to have jobs at the moment. They both left school early. I suppose I was thinking like most Travellers then, that they would get a bit of education, come out, get a job or make some kind of a living for themselves and settle down. Not so long ago, it wasn't all that easy or simple to get a job and my thinking was that if you had a chance of getting a job you took the job because in the long run it would benefit you more. Things at present are still not ideal regarding getting jobs, from the Travellers point of view, because due to poor reading and writing some employers are still reluctant to take on Travellers. Nevertheless there have been small improvements. I would say to any young Traveller person that education is important because a lot of change is going to take place for Travellers in the future and in a lot more ways that will make an education even more necessary to them.

Travellers and education – the way forward

Increased Traveller involvement

Travellers nowadays are thankfully becoming more vocal and expressing more openly what they want for their children from schools. They are more prepared with a bit of encouragement, to go to their child's school and express their concerns with teachers and principals. Some schools are more open to listening to parents and trying to change some of their practices. It will take time; it may even take another generation. The development of the home-school liaison system is another good idea whereby you have a link between the schools and families.

Changes in policy

At many different levels the whole area of education is being looked at. The Education Bill will be coming out in the near future and this will have an impact not only on Travellers but on settled people as well. We have too many young people from both communities, as has been our experience in Finglas, dropping out of school at far too early age and not doing anything else when they could be getting a fairly good education by staying on until fifteen or sixteen.

Tackling educational disadvantage

Educational disadvantage is now recognised as a key factor influencing a young person's life chances. The most recent ESRI figures (1997) indicate that 61% of young people who leave school with no qualifications are unemployed one year later. The Department of Education and Science estimates that in addition to the 2,200 pupils who left second-level education with no qualifications, a further 900 pupils did not transfer to second-level. What is even more alarming about these statistics is that according to them, a significant number of those who do not transfer to second-level are Travellers.

Positive discrimination for Travellers in schools

If a Traveller child drops out of school most of the blame is put on the child and the family but the fact is that because they are Travellers they don't seem to value education. At the same time however if you're being ignored and people aren't showing an interest in you then it's easy for you to feel that you don't have a part to play in school and you don't need to be there. For too long in the past Travellers have been let drop out without any positive follow up and this has led to Travellers feeling that they were not wanted because nobody was interested in them.

In one local secondary school in Finglas where most of the Traveller children attend, if a Traveller is absent for any length of time the home-community person will come down to the site talk to the parents and encourage the child to go back into the school. The home-liaison person can support the parents in fulfilling their responsibility to the child, who should be in school until a certain age. The fact that the home-liaison officer will make the effort and come down to the halting site, sit in the trailer, talk to the family of the young person and encourage them to return back to the school shows that the school is genuinely interested in the child. This can work because it shows Travellers that they are important and valued in the school.

Young Travellers
experience of school

Trainees of St. Joseph's Training Centre

How do Travellers experience education?

This is the question that we are hoping to address in our article. We come to this task as a group of young Traveller women presently attending St. Joseph's Training Centre in Finglas. Most of us have been through the Primary school system, from beginning to end, but some of us have only attended "on and off".

To present our experience of school we recorded two discussion sessions on this topic. Fr. Paddy Kelly facilitated the discussions and put together the following summary based on these discussions. While this article only represents our particular experience, we feel sure that many Travellers will be able to identify with it. It is also our hope that it will provide insights into Travellers' experience of education and schooling that will be both enlightening and helpful to those working with Travellers in any capacity.

The preference for "integrated" classes as opposed to "special" classes.

Most Travellers have spent some time in Primary school. Many go through and complete their education in one school. Travellers' experience of education is varied, depending especially on whether they are placed in a "mixed" (Traveller and settled) class or in a "special" Traveller class.

Brigid explains:

> I went to a school in Belfast. It was an " all Traveller" school and I liked it. The teachers were very nice. It was the school for the site that I was in. I went to it for about three years and I hardly learned anything, just a few words. I think if I'd gone to a settled school I'd have learned more. It was mostly all messing with the Travellers and that's why there was no work done. You weren't coming on in yourself. If you had been in a settled class you'd be more organised because you'd be down to your work. You'd watch the settled children do their work and you'd do yours as well. I'd send my children to a settled school because I think they'd learn more.

Lisa agrees:

> It's better that Travellers be mixed in with the settled children because today children are more chatty and confident within themselves than we were some years ago. And things have changed because there's a lot of talk about Travellers today and people know more about them and they are better able to mix today, Travellers and settled.

Geraldine elaborates further:

> I went to a mixture of schools. First I was in an all settled class. Then I went to Cavan to stay with my grandfather and grandmother for a month or something. When I came back my teacher said "you can go into the all Traveller class". I was unhappy in myself doing that and if I could turn back the clock I would have waited in the settled class because I know I'd have learned more. When you go into an "all Traveller" class it's all English and Maths and they're not bothered. But if you go into a settled class you have to learn History, Geography, Irish, English, Maths, Arts and Crafts,

Computers and all that.

Sometimes Traveller children come to school from camps that are totally without facilities of any kind. Sometimes, as in Sandra's case, the school responds by providing showers:

> In my school the Travelling children were dragged out of their classes at breaktime and brought in for a shower. That was terrible. You'd go down and you'd come back up and your hair would be all wet and you'd be in uniform. It was a show! You didn't have to go to these showers but it was only after a while that you got to know that.

The detrimental effects of low teacher expectations

Jacqueline called for equality of treatment for Travellers.

> Teachers should stop singling Travellers out. Make them do the same thing a settled person is doing. In my class all the settled girls would do Irish and I was put down doing an English essay. She didn't make me do the Irish as well. I was glad she didn't make me but she should have.

As many Travellers move from one area to another, some quite frequently, problems are raised for the school but often the Traveller child is the one who suffers most because teachers might be inclined to give up on them.

The effects of nomadism on schooling

Kathleen explains:

> I went to lots of schools because we travelled a lot. Coming and going didn't cause problems for me. It might have for the schools I went to. But the teacher never knew when we were going to move. We didn't even know it ourselves! If they did know they might leave you in a corner and not teach you at all.

Travelling often means that children will lose out on a lot of schooling. This can make the school even less attractive for the Traveller child. Brigid sums up the experience:

> Settled people are going to school all their lives but Traveller children miss out on half their schooling and they can find it all beyond them.

The need for an intercultural curriculum

A weakness in the school attended by Maire was the absence of any input on Traveller culture:

You'd never hear of teachers talking about Travellers' ways and helping children understand something of how Travellers live. Settled children should know where Travellers come from. History is all about country people. There's very little about Travellers – except that they come from the famine, or something like that.

Pauline, who spent some time in secondary school, identified the same weakness there:

If teachers know at the beginning of the year that there's going to be Travellers or Pakistanis or whatever in the class – they should have subjects in their heads – what to do and what not to do with them. Because there's all kind of people coming into classes now and they need to know more about one another and not be looking at one another as if they were aliens.

The futility of school

Although Marie describes primary school as "alright", she says:

I did hate coming into school – being there all day. No point saying I didn't. Being stuck in the one place all day puts Travellers off and you get nothing out of it at the end of it. No matter how much we went to school not one of us has a good job.

The pain of isolation

Sandra gives her experience:

I went to Secondary school for a month. There were no Travellers, only me. The girls would chat to you alright but I had no interest in them. I just didn't want to be there and I had to get out. It is hard for one Traveller but if you had just one more with you you'd stick it for a while longer I'd say.

Pauline tried Secondary school for a little longer but eventually left too. The different lifestyle of her settled peers and their constant topics of conversation were too far from her experience. The pressure was too much.

Primary school was alright. It was secondary school that turned me off. I didn't like it because it was only me and my sister and there were no other Travellers. The country girls used to talk about boys and parties and whatever else and you couldn't join with them in conversation. You ended up just sitting there, letting on you were doing everything but you were doing nothing. If I was back again I'd stay and lie my way right through to sixth year, letting on I was going to parties as well.

Lisa emphasised the loneliness of a Traveller in secondary school:

School was a bad experience for me because there was only one Traveller in class with me and to tell you the truth I didn't like going one bit. The rest of the girls left you there on your own. They didn't want to chat to you – so you were just left there by yourself. If I had the confidence I'd have talked to them but I hadn't so I didn't bother. If I was back again I wouldn't be ashamed or feel that I was lower than them because I know I'm not.

Pauline expressed the loneliness in a different way:

I thought that everyone was staring at us because we were the only Travellers in the class.

Traveller girls "more mature" than their settled peers

Lisa believes that not only are Travellers well able to do the work they're given but that they are actually more mature than settled girls of the same age.

When Traveller girls go into school and when country girls go into school, teachers don't realise it but they might be the one age but the Travelling girls are more far on – like, when the father and mother go off they mind the children, they know how to wash the vessels (see glossary) and that kind of thing. Country girls, in my opinion, haven't even come up to that stage yet. Travelling girls are a lot more mature than country girls. Teachers don't realise that Travelling girls come from a home where she's minding children and washing vessels and things like that.

Pauline agrees and gives a practical example to emphasise Lisa's point:

You know when you go into hospital to have a child and the nurse comes around. They think you're real foolish, that you don't know how to change a child, you don't know how to feed her right. They go round for to help the country women especially with their first babies. They say to me: "How old are you?" I tell them and they say "Look how good you can cope with your baby. Look how you can change and feed it and get up its wind real quick". Swear to God, they haven't got a clue that Travellers are doing this since they were children.

Lisa points out that this experience in the home is often at the expense of homework:

Country girls go home and go out and play whereas Travellers go home and can't do their homework because they've too much to do. Teachers think all they have to do is to go home and go out playing all day. It's not like that at all.

The role of parental attitudes

Jacqueline recalls her school days in Navan and her parents' easy-going attitude to her education:

> I went to school in Navan and I was the only Traveller in the class. I used to mix with the girls. There was an odd one of them that would talk behind your back and call you names. I left school in fifth class. I didn't go any higher than that. Travellers leave after confirmation because they're let leave. Parents should make their children go on to secondary school. I just said I was dropping out and that was grand. There was no saying "you're going back to school" or anything like that. You know anyway that you're going to get engaged and girls come out of school to get married.

Jacqueline's mother was not impressed however by the effect Secondary school was having on her other daughter, as Jacqueline says:

> My sister was very brainy and got on very well at school. My mother wanted her out of school because, to her, she was getting too cheeky from mixing with the country girls, wanting to go to parties and all that. So Winnie says "your coming out, your going to no parties". She was coming out to get married anyway but Winnie was glad she was coming out.

Geraldine was inclined to agree with Jacqueline's mother but went on to express her perception of the problem in the following way:

> Even if I asked to go to secondary school I wouldn't be let. My mother would get me up every morning for primary school but as for secondary school – she wouldn't like that at all. She wouldn't let her young ones go to places like that and to tell you the truth I think that she is right. Young ones who go to secondary school change into something that they're not. They're acting like country people. They're dressing like country people. They don't like jewellery no more. They don't like being a Traveller no more. They don't change in a good way. They're trying to be something that they're not. The point I'm making – the way you go in is the way you should come out with plenty of education but still proud to be a Traveller.

The changes brought about by full-time education, a benefit or threat to Traveller identity ?

Change was accepted as a good and necessary result of education. But what was the nature of the change? Was it a change that strengthened a young person's identity as a Traveller or was it a change that represented a serious loss. Winnie was in no doubt:

> Sometimes educated Travellers go on television and I don't know from A to Z what they're saying and I've heard an awful lot of people saying it. What's the point? If I'm educated or I come in here and you don't know what I'm on about you'd get sick of me.

Nonetheless education was accepted as vital for Travellers in the future. Despite the varied change it caused in individual Travellers, Lisa was still confident of its positive power:

> I think that if you rear your child to be confident about her culture and to be confident enough in school, she'll get her education and still come back to be a Traveller.

Hopes for the future

Lisa was quite sure about what she wanted for hers:

> I'd like to see my child go on to secondary school and if she doesn't want to go I will force her into it, 'til I know she has had enough education got. Because in 16 or 17 years time things will have changed completely and marriage will be put back for a good while and I'd rather see her have a good education first, a good job and then she can settle down and get married.

Winnie was less sure:

> I don't know what I want for my child. I'd let her go through primary school and if she didn't want to go on to secondary school I wouldn't send her on. In 20 years time I'd like to see her having a good job and being well -off and happy. School would help that by giving her a good education, giving her confidence and things like that.

Caroline had her hopes but was equally aware that her children could not be forced:

> I would send my child to secondary school so that they'd have different things from what I have, a good job, a good education and not to get married so young. I'd tell them to go but I suppose that if they didn't really want to go you couldn't really force them.

All the girls wanted 'more' for their children than they got themselves. As Jacqueline says:

> I would send my child to secondary school. It would give her a better

chance. I'm a very bad reader and I can barely write. It would give her a chance to do something better, wouldn't it?

To achieve this 'more', education was seen to be vital. Despite their mixed experience of education and schooling, all expressed the hope that through it a better future could be had for their children, a future that would strengthen their identity as Travellers, open up new possibilities and give them the confidence to grasp those opportunities with courage and enthusiasm.

The Irish Traveller Movement

Thomas McCann

ITM - Its Role and Relationship With Other Traveller Organisations

The Irish Traveller Movement (ITM) was founded in 1990. It is a national network of Traveller organisations, local Traveller support groups, and individuals working within the Traveller community. ITM has in its membership over seventy Traveller organisations from all parts of the island of Ireland, and is in contact with Traveller groups in Britain. The ITM consists of a partnership of Travellers and settled people committed to addressing the harsh living circumstances in which Travellers are forced to live. Members are united in their common understanding of Travellers as a distinct ethnic group in Irish society, for whom nomadism is very important. The ITM provides Travellers and their organisations with a national platform to:

- highlight the problems of Travellers and to press for real solutions.

- draft and promote new, culturally-appropriate, policy initiatives.

- provide individuals and groups who are active at a local level with support and solidarity.

- develop national level alliances.

Membership and management structures of the ITM

Traveller organisations are defined as organisations which have Traveller representatives on their management structures. These groups are full members of the ITM and can vote in electing people onto the central group in the ITM. Associate members, whether individuals or affiliated organisations, such as The Association of Teachers of Travellers and the Visiting Teacher Service, fulfil different roles but are affiliated with the ITM in the shared struggle to achieve recognition of Travellers as an ethnic minority and to eliminate racism towards Travellers. (The structure of the ITM can be seen in Fig. 1)

Each year an election to the central group is held which tries to achieve a widespread representation from the thirty-two counties, with fourteen people elected from the local groups onto the central group who also elect the chairperson. For that year the central group directs policy, oversees the work of the staff, meets on a monthly basis to evaluate work through feedback and gives policy direction in terms of fulfilling the aims and objectives set out.

In addition to this there are also seven national sub-groups, which are concerned with issues such as Education, Accommodation, Anti-discrimination, Youth, Legislation, Health and finally there is a sub-group on Horses. Meetings of these groups are held throughout the country, in efforts to link local people into a national action or national policy development. There are also regional development networks. For example, we have an East Coast network and a Southern network, which are composed of the groups along the Eastern and Southern coasts and which try to assist weaker groups in their areas in terms of providing resources and support. We are also at present in the process of developing the Western network.

In terms of my own work in the ITM, I am currently the National Development Worker. My role involves supporting local groups by identifying their needs and the issues of the local people and looking at how these needs might be met and how the aims that they have set out might be achieved. In brief, my job involves developing local capacity and then linking the local into the national but it also involves making sure that there is local representation of Travellers at national structures and on local authorities.

The role of settled people in Traveller organisations and the need for greater Traveller involvement in these organisations

The role of settled people varies in different groups. In the ITM we have a partnership approach i.e. settled and Traveller working together, as equals, with a shared goal in mind. Settled people have most definitely played a significant part, as equal players, in the development of Traveller organisations. In some local groups there is a lot of Traveller participation, at the worker as well as at the management level, but unfortunately in other groups there is not, especially when it is in regard to Traveller representation at the management level. There are a number of reasons for this, the main one being that although these groups want more Traveller involvement, it can be difficult to recruit Travellers in certain areas depending on the number of Travellers in those areas.

We in the ITM try to encourage and develop the capacity of groups for more Traveller involvement mainly by making involvement more accessible for Travellers. As part of our role we facilitate groups by having meetings on the sites, making sure that Travellers are getting the information that they need, establishing contact people and engaging in other such endeavours. The fact is that there is a lot more Traveller involvement in the last ten years than ever before and the success of this is mainly due to the strategies that local groups are

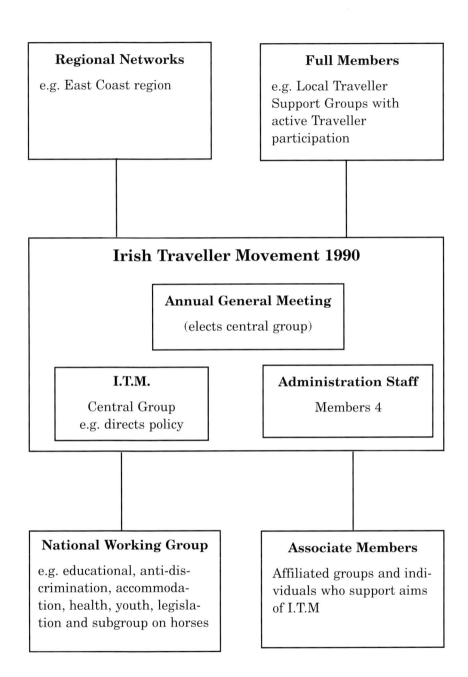

Fig. 1

coming up with. Such strategies include engaging in local area profiles to identify people who might become involved and then trying to acquire and provide the necessary resources.

Some of the key factors in establishing involvement include; trying to tailor some of the courses and the schemes with Travellers in mind, trying to get the resources to employ Travellers on an equal basis and creating more jobs for Travellers through the partnership companies. Traveller organisations need Traveller involvement at every level, particularly at management level. What settled people are trying to do may be very acceptable but the way in which it might be done might differ slightly when you have Travellers involved, and might just mean that more Travellers would respond positively, (to the initiative or event etc.), because you've just got that bit closer to where they are coming from.

Achievements made by Traveller organisations

• Greater participation by Traveller men

There has always been an involvement of a minority of men but there has been a gradual increase and we need to look at ways in which we can encourage this shift. One of the factors behind women's involvement has been the fact that the courses, (which were ANCO courses in the past but which are now FAS courses) were mainly taken up by women because it wouldn't affect their dole, but if a man went on the course it would affect his dole so that discouraged men's participation and I think that this needs to be looked at. It seems however, that men are becoming more involved at the local and national levels and it is not just the women all the time. Nevertheless, there is still a need for greater participation from Traveller men.

• Improvements in the areas of accommodation and employment

Some other achievements, in addition to the increase in Traveller involvement at a local level, include the increase in negotiations between Travellers and local authorities in determining the kind of accommodation that should be provided. In terms of employment, schemes such as the local employment scheme, the CE schemes and the partnership companies, have all been successful in influencing their strategic plans and in acquiring resources for youth and women's courses.

• Successful health initiatives

In addition to this, there has also been a huge development right across the country, in the area of health, in terms of the Health Boards establishing specific committees to research and improve Travellers' health. These achievements confirm that a huge shift at the national level, supported by legislation and by people negotiating at the national level, has taken place. One of the key factors in this shift has been the publication and implementation of the recommendations of the *The Report of the Task Force on the Travelling Community 1995*, which set the scene for this to happen.

• Relationship-building

The key factor in increasing the participation of Travellers, whether it is in the workplace or in their local parishes, is the building up of relationships.

Building up a relationship with local Travellers and making sure that things are structured to encourage participation so that it is not organised in such a way that makes it more difficult for people to participate are vital. Giving people the space to have input is also important.

• Accountability Of Traveller Organisations

In regard to accountability, organisations that are providing services that are responding to the needs of Travellers, (based on research on the ground), need to make these services accessible to the wider Traveller Community, by constantly reviewing their services and by actively encouraging greater Traveller participation. In this way these organisations are being as accountable as they can be.

Difficulties facing Traveller support groups – obstacles to progress

• Resources

There are a number of difficulties for support groups, one of the main ones however is the area of resources. Most groups face a constant struggle to acquire resources for buildings, to set up an office, or even just to hire a worker because, although people may offer their services voluntarily for a while, someone is still needed to do the work on the ground on a day-to-day basis.

• Capacity-building

Another area of difficulty is the area of capacity-building at local level, because failure to do so results in limitation of involvement. Capacity-building means developing certain abilities in people, such as the ability not merely to interact but to initiate. It also involves developing skills – community development skills, youth work skills, negotiation skills (e.g. in dealing with local authorities), media skills, and a whole variety of other skills – all of which are needed in working with people at a local level.

• Discrimination

Discrimination however remains the biggest obstacle to progress, because Travellers in negotiating with other people are oftentimes faced with exclusion from the process, even when they are putting their case across. You can see it very clearly, with the accommodation committees at local authority level, when Travellers experience exclusion from discussions and this is one of the biggest blocks. I believe however that once the doors are open, even a little, it will be easier for progress to be made and for better things to happen.

• Inadequate accommodation

In terms of accommodation needs at local level, it is very difficult for Travellers to become involved on an equal basis in the process of negotiations or in society, if they are living in a field and they have no electricity or running water.

• Lack of education

Education is another difficulty because if people are being denied the right to be educated or if it is being offered in a way that doesn't cater for their needs, then once again they are being excluded from developing their full potential.

• Threat to Traveller economy

I also think that in regard to employment, it has become harder and harder, particularly for Travellers, to carry on traditional ways of making a living, whether that is recycling or horse dealing. Horses have been a part of Travellers' lives for generations and now there is a new Horses' Bill which creates a further difficulty for Travellers. All of these realities limit Traveller participation in Irish society.

• Social exclusion

In addition to these difficulties there is also the social aspect of life in the local communities where, despite the fact that Travellers have been living twenty or thirty years in an area, they are still not seen as local, either by the local authority or by the local people. They are viewed as outsiders. There is an attitudinal change that needs to happen, because even though people may not openly discriminate against Travellers, they are discriminating against them by refusing to recognise them as local people. Even in regard to local parishes, Travellers wouldn't be seen as parishioners, but as outsiders.

• Refusal of services

In the area of services, it is harder for local Travellers to build up a relationship with their settled neighbours when they are not getting the same goods and services as their neighbours are. Services include not only access to pubs but also being able to book a hotel for a wedding or to enter a shop without being followed around or to use public transport. These very basic services that settled people take for granted are refused to Travellers. It's embarrassing if you walk into the laundrette in your local area and if they say, "aah, sorry, we're all full up for the next . . ." and that has happened a few times. I think that one of the things that needs to happen is that the Equal Status legislation should to be brought in. I am on the Equality Authority and hopefully that will put an infrastructure in place that people can use, that Travellers will use.

Attitudinal change has to happen in society in order for us to benefit from the legislation, because you don't want people to be reluctantly providing you services simply because they have to, you want them to feel easy about going in and getting a service.

Bringing about attitudinal change

• Raising awareness

Traveller groups raising public awareness about the issues concerning Travellers is one major way to bring about attitudinal change. This involves responding to newspaper and radio requests giving Travellers' side of the story so that people become more aware of what is going on. The church is also a key player in the local area in raising awareness and in promoting attitudinal change. There is a lot of work to be done but having said that, progress has been and is being made.

• Promoting recognition of Travellers as full equal citizens of Ireland with a distinct culture

Traveller groups also have a role, to varying degrees depending on the nature of their work, to assist in meeting the cultural needs of Travellers. This means encouraging the celebration of Traveller identity and the development of self-esteem, by valuing the contribution which Travellers have made to Irish society, a contribution that is not fully recognised. These groups also have a responsibility to strive for the recognition of Travellers as full citizens of Ireland. Resourcing and recognising Traveller culture and helping Travellers to take pride in it is to be encouraged because Traveller culture has been seen to be very negative. Some Travellers, especially younger ones, see their culture as something to be denied. The result is that there is a huge wealth of culture on the verge of being lost unless it is developed and resourced.

Events that led to my involvement with the ITM

• Anger – a creative force

A number of things led to my involvement with the ITM. Firstly, I'm a Traveller and I have experienced first-hand what it is like to be discriminated against and to see my immediate family discriminated against. This gives you a feeling of helplessness, that there is nothing you can do about it, that you just have to accept the way things are. In some ways not only were you discriminated against and excluded, but you were punched as well, so I always had a feeling that something needed to be done about this. It was through a kind of anger that something needed to be done that my involvement began. One of the key moments for me was the march in Tallaght in regard to the by-pass. Through this event I became involved in a whole range of activities. Back then, there were no resources, people were threatened with being put off the dole because they weren't available for work, and Travellers were being seen as troublemakers. It was a difficult time but through Traveller demonstrations and protests, when for the first time Travellers came out marching on the streets, a sense of empowerment began to emerge and other changes started to happen.

• Education

It was also through courses that people began to become more involved. I went to Maynooth and did a Community Development course and brought the experience of that back and other people saw this course as an opening they could use because it is also creating opportunities for Travellers. Initially, when Travellers became involved, it was very difficult at times for them as they were subject to a lot of slagging. I won't call it "abuse", but it certainly wasn't encouragement and, because Travellers weren't getting paid for the course they weren't being encouraged to become involved. Nevertheless, we had to overcome a number of obstacles. I, along with others, had to try and channel our anger in a constructive rather than a destructive way. Now, I'm glad now that we've channelled it because you do need energy to keep going after all these years.

• Greater awareness of the need for equality

Other groups became very much involved with the issue of equality and this was a support and still is. Within the voluntary and community sector Travellers have had a leading role in developing that sector around other groups, people with disabilities and refugees and asylum seekers, the whole anti-racist agenda. We've played a role in trying to keep a broad campaign rather than just seeing the issue as being "only a Traveller issue" - there are some issues that relate only to Travellers but many issues relate to other groups.

Travellers and other ethnic minorities – building relationships

• Solidarity – the key to equality

When you are trying to eradicate poverty and create equality, when you are trying to create social justice with other people, the unemployed, working class people, black people and people with disabilities, there's a huge need for equality for so many different groups. This broad campaign for equality is something that I would like to see continuing to develop. Solidarity I think is a key word when we are talking about Travellers and we need to create that solidarity with other groups. It is my opinion that we've achieved a lot in this regard, not only here in Ireland, but also at the European level.

• Travellers In Europe – building solidarity

The ITM has always had involvement in the Romany union - we've had a representative for the last fifteen years, but in the last six to seven years there has been more development with other groups, both indigenous Travellers from other countries, and also Romany groups from other countries, and we're trying to build up solidarity. There hasn't been solidarity even among some of the Romany groups. It was very difficult with six or seven different groups in some countries. It wasn't unlike our own situation ten or fifteen years ago. It can be very difficult for them to come together in solidarity and we played a fairly active role in trying to do that. Recently, we had a conference in Belgium where we brought most of the Gypsy leaders together including ourselves and tried to present a model of moving forward at a European level. Hopefully, the next step to come out of this will be starting a number of developments between groups in Ireland and other Gypsy groups around not only Western Europe but Eastern Europe as well. Also there has been an increase in contact not just among the Romany people but also between organisations that represent European human rights.

Building relationships between mainstream groups and Travellers groups through exchanges both at youth level but also at a more political level, at the European parliament or the Council of Europe, has been a key concern and an achievement. Organisationally we've done much better because of the model that we've used and there are a number of initiatives coming on stream that will be welcomed in terms of getting normal groups involved such as the European Centre for Monitoring Racism and the European Anti-Racist Network.

We are probably going to see a more organisational capacity in the other countries and that will feed into a much stronger organisation at the European level. The key element is building solidarity.

I think that there is a need to get rid of the idea that indigenous nomadic groups, although they may not strictly belong to Romany, are not equally entitled to the same rights to become involved in organising. The fact is that we share many customs such as a nomadic way of life, a similar lifestyle etc. throughout the world, even though there may be different languages, traditions, or religions.

It is another development that now these indigenous nomadic groups are beginning to get organised so not only do you have the Romany population in most countries but you now have the indigenous nomadic groups organising and there are a number of examples of where this is happening. Our relationship with Romany Gypsies is building up, but it takes time.

The way forward

Creating an egalitarian society

My hope is for society to become more equitable and that there would be a more even distribution of wealth so that there wouldn't be a need for people to be involved – I would love not to have to go out and fight our corner. I would love to have an ordinary job, do ordinary things but unfortunately the situation doesn't allow for that and either you accept it or else you do something about it. Also, I think a lot of people felt that there was a need to do something about the situation of Travellers. Many of the people who are involved in Travellers' issues aren't employed, a lot of the work is being done voluntarily and there's a huge need to resource the work, as one of the huge struggles is to get resources all the time. The more people that get involved in anti-poverty work and social justice work the better. In terms of what Emmett Stagg has termed "the poverty industry", I suggest that we drop this idea of industry and eradicate poverty. That's where we should all be putting our energy.

I would hope that I have had an influence on the way things have progressed and I am glad of where we've got to now. I think that we have moved a long way and that in some ways I have influenced that. I would also hope that we in the ITM have had a wider influence, along with other Traveller groups around the country, on the whole community sector.

Accommodation, Education, Health

Now that the Traveller Accommodation Legislation is going through, every local authority in the country has to have a Local Accommodation Consultative Group, which is going to create huge changes. In addition to this, at Departmental level there is a co-ordinating committee looking at the whole area of accommodation which we, in the ITM, have representatives on.

In regard to the issue of education there is an advisory committee in the Department of Education, which again we have representatives on. This committee plans to look at the whole area of education.

In the Department of Health there will be a national health strategy that will come out and will influence how healthcare is provided to Travellers, addressing the major issues and ways to tackle them. This strategy will also have an input into local Health Boards in terms of delivering that service and employed in it in terms of healthcare workers, will be the equality agenda which is about to open up in terms of Travellers.

Equal Status Legislation

In addition to this there is also an Equality Authority which has been set up to assess the structure to ensure that people can have their grievances heard. The Equal Status legislation and the Employment *Equality Act* came into operation on the eighteenth of October 1999 when the Equality Authority was implemented, which also consists of representatives from the ITM. There is a monitoring body set up to ensure that the recommendations of *The Report of the Task Force on the Travelling Community 1995*, especially in the legislative area, are enforced.

There are still some issues that need to be addressed. One of these is the whole social economy and Travellers making of a living which needs to be resourced. I know there are downsides and that it's not all going to be rosy, but I definitely think that these developments are going to have huge benefits for Travellers.

CITIZEN TRAVELLER
supporting Travellers as an ethnic group

A partnership of four Traveller organisations

1. Citizen Traveller Campaign

◆ The Citizen Traveller Campaign has been developed by a partnership of four organisations working with the Traveller Community in Ireland. These organisations are, the Irish Traveller Movement, the Parish of the Travelling People, Pavee Point and the National Traveller Women's Forum.

◆ The four member Traveller partnership has been allocated £900,000 from the Department of Justice, Equality and Law Reform to fund a three-year communications campaign. This money was allocated in the budget of December 1998 and the campaign became a reality with the appointment of a full-time administrator in June 1999 and the official launch in October.

◆ Funding was granted to the four member Traveller partnership following a lobbying campaign to the government by its members and with the voluntary assistance of individuals working within the media / marketing industry.

◆ The main objective of Citizen Traveller is to develop a three year campaign to support the work of Traveller organisations in creating a better understanding between the settled and Traveller communities in Ireland, creating an environment to promote Travellers as equal citizens in Irish society and encouraging the Traveller community to take pride in their own cultural identity.

◆ The campaign will be directed at the Traveller and settled community alike and at a range of other broad-reaching audiences including, social, religious, commercial and public service groups. Funding for the three years will be used to develop a series of planned public education and awareness programmes incorporating media relations, advertising and direct marketing, public affairs and research. Three marketing and communications agencies will work in conjunction with Citizen Traveller to create projects focused on public education and awareness.

♦ Citizen Traveller has been designed to address the imbalance in the relationship between the Traveller and settled communities and in the first year will focus on and highlight the issues of accommodation and discrimination.

♦ On all levels the campaign has been developed with assistance and input from the Traveller Community.

♦ The advertising campaign will encompass the use of radio, outdoor and print. Direct marketing will be used to target specific audiences with specific pieces of information relative to the campaign objectives

♦ The public relations campaign will address pertinent issues through a number of initiatives and in the first year will include a week long media focus on Travellers, media training and ongoing media relations exercises to promote the visibility and participation of Travellers in Irish society.

♦ Research will play an important part of the overall campaign and in part will serve to establish current attitudes and behaviour among the settled and Traveller communities.

2. Citizen Traveller member organisations

The Parish of the Travelling People

In 1980 the Vincentian Community was asked by the Archbishop of Dublin to respond to the pastoral needs of the Traveller community throughout the diocese.

The Parish's response to the Traveller community who are excluded from Irish society is one of solidarity and partnership. Our work prompts us to act as agents of change, working with Travellers to have their rights realized and facilitating their full participation as equals in the church and in society.

We resource local parishes in efforts to build relationships between the Traveller and settled people at a local level and to ensure the participation of parishioners, both Traveller and settled, in the life and activities of parishes.

Contact: Parish of the Travelling People, 6 New Cabra Road, Dublin 7

Tel: 01 838 8874 Fax: 01 838 8901 E-mail: partravs@iol.ie

The National Traveller Women's Forum

The National Traveller Women's Forum is an alliance of Traveller women and Traveller organisations from throughout Ireland, which aims to:

Work collectively to challenge the racism and sexism experienced by Traveller women and promote Traveller women's right to self determination, the attainment of human rights and equality within society.

The work of the National Traveller Women's Forum involves:

◆ Policy work

◆ Lobbying and Campaigning

◆ Training and Capacity Building

◆ Information Dissemination and Exchange

◆ Annual Forum Days

◆ Networking

◆ Support

Contact: National Traveller Women's Forum, 1st Floor, Unit 4, Tuam Road Centre, Tuam Road, Galway

Tel: 091 771 509 Fax: 091 771235 E-mail: ntwf@iol.ie

Irish Traveller Movement

The Irish Traveller Movement (ITM) was founded in 1990. It is a national network of organisations and individuals working within the Traveller community. ITM has in its membership over 70 Traveller organisations from all parts of the island of Ireland, and extends to contact with Traveller groups in Britain. The ITM consists of a partnership of Travellers and settled people committed to seeking full equality for Travellers in Irish society. This partnership is reflected in all ITM structures. ITM seeks to give a 'voice' to Travellers in national, social and economic policy arenas.

Contact: Irish Traveller Movement, 4-5 Eustace Street, Dublin 2

Tel: 01 6796577   Fax: 01 6796578   E-mail: itmtrav@indigo.ie

Pavee Point

Pavee Point is a non-governmental organisation, which is committed to human rights for Irish Travellers. The group comprises Travellers and members of the majority population working together in partnership to address the needs of Travellers as a minority group which experiences exclusion and marginalisation.

The work of Pavee Point is based on two key promises:

◆ Real improvement in Travellers living circumstances and social situation requires active involvement of Travellers themselves.

◆ Non-Travellers have a responsibility to address the widespread prejudice, discrimination and racism which prevent Travellers from participating as equals in society.

Pavee Point acknowledges the distinct culture of Travellers and the importance of nomadism to the Traveller way of life. The group seeks to combine local action with national resourcing and direct work with research and policy formulation.

Contact: Pavee Point, 46 North Great Charles Street, Dublin 1

Tel: 01 878 0255   Fax: 01 874 2626   E-Mail: Pavee@iol.ie

Website: http://homepages.iol.ie/~pavee/

Challenges to Irish society

Frank Murphy C.M.

I have been working in the Parish of the Travelling People for the past six years. Compiling this book has been an exciting and rewarding task as in a way, it is for me the fruit of these very challenging and meaningful years. I have had my eyes opened to the beauty and dignity of a people I had only known in very limited ways in the past. Nevertheless, from my previous experiences I knew that the directness and honesty of Travellers would enrich me. This has proven to be the case and it has been very refreshing to experience the lack of veneer and image that seems to be so much part of settled society. I recall a Traveller woman who, on a visit to President Mary Robinson was looking at the President's bracelet and said, "Mary, is that real gold or imitation gold? "The President enjoyed that as much as I did. There is no façade and what you see is what you get. This quality Christ praised Nathaniel for, when he described him as a man "in whom there is nothing false".

The rights of Travellers as full 'equal' citizens

Travellers are full citizens of Ireland but they are not treated as equal citizens because their basic human rights are denied them on a daily basis. Travellers must be given the recognition of their neglected human rights in the Ireland of the 21st century. We have the resources but have we the courage and political will to make this recognition happen? The rights that need to be respected include;

◆ The Right to Cultural Respect

'Culture and cultural respect is an important right of people within every society' (*CORI Resources and Choices 1999*). Yet, the history of our treatment of Travellers in Irish society has been to deny them this cultural respect and in so doing we are denying Travellers their very identity and right to exist. Far from valuing and appreciating the values that a different culture could enrich Ireland with, we have systematically persecuted and excluded the Traveller community through our prejudicial attitudes and laws, and through our education, accommodation and health care policies. The challenge now facing Ireland is to create a society in which Travellers and the other ethnic minorities are respected and affirmed as valued members of our society.

◆ The right to sufficient income to live with basic dignity

◆ The right to work

◆ The right to appropriate accommodation

◆ The right to basic health care

◆ The right to relevant education

◆ The right to participate in the cultural life and heritage of the community and wider society. (This includes the right of minorities to have their cultures respected.)

◆ The right to participate in shaping the decisions that affect their lives.

(CORI Resources and Choices 1999)

This CORI document puts before us a challenge to "to seek out and articulate a vision of the future in which everyone has full citizenship". If our society is to be egalitarian, which according to the recent survey taken by the Irish Times/MRBI poll (November 6, 1999) is what Irish people want, then we need to commit ourselves to responding to this challenge.

Equality of condition

Equality of treatment for all citizens is enshrined in our Constitution. For an egalitarian society to develop there needs to be "equality of condition". Equality of condition means equal distribution of wealth, resources, power and privilege for all members of society, so that members of all groups can be in a position to make real choices and have equal access to accommodation, health care, education etc

As Travellers are suffering from extreme conditions of disadvantage, due in particular to the extremely poor accommodation in which they are forced to live and to the daily experience of discrimination, equality of condition is an absolute must. In addition to this, there is also the financial, social, cultural and educational disadvantage highlighted in the document by the Clondalkin Travellers Development Group when, in exploring the barriers preventing Travellers accessing second- level education, it points out that,

> The issues facing Travellers cannot be seen in isolation from the many factors affecting their quality of life, inappropriate accommodation which often impacts on Travellers' ability to engage effectively in the education process. Poor health and the everyday experiences of discrimination on a personal and institutional level. All of these factors must be considered when engaging in any real dialogue on the education of Travellers.
>
> *(Clondalkin Travellers Development Group 1998)*

We, as members of a thriving and prosperous society, are challenged to ensure that the rising tide of our present economic boom is indeed lifting all boats.

Achieving equality – addressing the issues

Accommodation

Never in my life as a priest have I felt as paralysed by the pain I experienced as when I, led the funeral mass of a young woman burnt in a fire or, attended the funerals of numerous young people whose deaths need not have been but were in some way related to the inhuman conditions in which they are forced to live by the settled community. These experiences are far from being isolated and have happened many times throughout my years in the Parish. It may be a harsh thing to say but it is hard not to draw the conclusion that we would prefer children to die rather than have them live near us in decent and suitable accommodation. As Michael McDonagh said :"When you use your power to stop any person from getting better facilities and living conditions you are contributing to them dying."

Understanding nomadism and combating the resettlement attitude

The first step to solving the accommodation crisis of Travellers is understanding and accepting nomadism. Nomadism is about your whole outlook on life and a different way of seeing and valuing family, freedom, enterprise and accommodation. "The Traveller is a nomad, even when he does not travel. Immobilised, he remains a Traveller. Whereas a sedentary person remains sedentary, even when travelling" (*Liégeois, Gypsies and Travellers 1987*). Nomadism has been part of civilisation from the beginning of time. Most countries have their own nomadic groups. In Europe it has been the Gypsies. In Ireland, the Travellers.

As settled people we have very little, if any, understanding of nomadism. The perception of most settled people is that Travellers are a problem which they hope will be solved through Travellers becoming "integrated" or "resettled" back into the settled community. One of the questions I am most often asked is "Are Travellers going to settle down"? Michael McDonagh has shown that this attitude towards Travellers today can be traced back to *The Itinerant Resettlement Commission of 1963* which tried to solve the "itinerant" problem by putting a stop to itinerancy, to nomadism. "The process was all wrong because it saw us as the problem. It didn't see us as people with accommodation problems". It also led to the setting up of the many "settlement" committees. This mentality has thankfully been replaced by the recognition in *the Task Force Report on the Travelling Community 1995* of the distinct cultural identity of the Travelling people.

Nevertheless, the damage done by the "resettlement" attitude is still the basic mind-set out of which most Irish people operate. In particular local councils demonstrate a blatant lack of comprehension in regard to nomadism in their systematic squeezing of Travellers in a pincer- like movement by continually bouldering up all possible halting sites while at the same time wilfully failing to provide alternative accommodation. Michael McDonagh in his article asks "In future, when we look at these boulders, will we see them as a monument to prejudice?" These boulders and mounds of earth are one of the powerful symbols of the Ireland of 2000, the Ireland of the Celtic tiger.

Local councils: – lack of will power in providing an adequate response

David Joyce points out that all the money that is needed to meet the accommodation needs of Travellers immediately has been available for many years now. The problem is that local councils have demonstrated a lack of will power by their failure to use the money available to them. This lack of will power can be contributed, in part, to the fear of many local councillors to face opposition from their constituents, despite the fact that,as Pat Brady in his article points out, when sites are built to a good standard and properly landscaped, local opposition evaporates and there is no identifiable effect on property values! As Michael McDonagh so succinctly said "People don't devalue property, attitudes do".

This lack of will power is further compounded by the fact that the Accommodation Section of Councils dealing with Traveller accommodation have suffered in many cases from a shortage of staff. Pat Brady said that the reason why only, 125 units of Traveller specific accommodation were provided in the years 1995-2000 as compared with the 3,100 promised by the Government in 1995, was that "there has been a failure to develop a corps of planners and administrators". The fact is that council employees do not stay long enough to become acquainted with the brief and more importantly to build a positive relationship with Travellers and   local Traveller support groups before moving on to another department. Travellers are in a "no win" situation. I have witnessed this lack of personnel in one Council and what makes the matter worse is the shockingly negative attitude of the people in power towards the Travellers for whom they are responsible.

Local councils: – refusal to recognise the existence of Travellers

1250 Traveller families have no place to live and are forced to settle on unofficial sites. The anger of local communities is directed at Travellers NOT at the Local Authorities who have systematically failed to provide accommodation for them. These same local authorities refuse to provide any refuse collection for these families. It is therefore very interesting to note that the Citizen Traveller survey also found that 93% of settled people agree with the statement that "Travellers leave a lot of rubbish wherever they stop". Wouldn't the same be true of any settled family if they too were refused any refuse collection ? The difference is that when it comes to settled people the local councils provide containers and/or pick up their rubbish but refuse to do it for Travellers who are nomadic.

I have had many personal experiences of councils in the Dublin area refusing to recognise Traveller families as existing because they have moved into the capital in the last two years. They term these Travellers "transient" or "traders" and claim that they have no obligation towards them because they are not "indigenous". In many cases they refuse to register them, even in their annual census of Travellers, in an effort to "lose" them so that they don't have to provide for them in their accommodation programmes because, in the eyes of the council officials, they don't exist! What would happen if settled people were told they could not get accommodation in Dublin if they were not resident here before 1997? Nevertheless, this is what is being said to many Traveller families.

Local councils: – the development of an "isolationist" policy

Over the last thirty-five years, Government policy towards Travellers has been a policy of "assimilation" which local authorities ignored and in practice put in place a policy of "isolation". With the publication of

The Report of the Task Force on the Travelling Community 1995, Government policy is now one of "respect for culture". But the implementation of this policy still rests in the hands of the local authorities. David Joyce rightly asks "Will the result be the same in that local authorities will continue to defy government policy by creating accommodation programmes at local level that continue to isolate Travellers?"

Given our present experience of how many councils are reacting to *The Housing (Traveller Accommodation) Act 1998* I believe that this is the most likely outcome, bearing in mind that as David Joyce points out, "there have been situations where Traveller representatives and members of the local community were told they couldn't even see the reports until they went public. Unfortunately, the majority of councils fitted into this more negative category.

Local councils: – lack of consultation with Travellers

The basic human right under the constitution to participate in shaping the decisions that affect your life is being denied to Travellers in the year 2000. The council that I have had closest contact with has behaved in a manner that I could only describe as outrageous and demeaning of the respect that any and every human being is entitled to in this regard. This surely is a major challenge to policy-makers at council level. Added to this is the fact that local councils have put enormous energy into Section 32 of the Act which has given them increased powers of eviction. This is a major concern because as David Joyce points out it,

> Highlights the real intentions of local authorities toward Traveller accommodation, which could be minimalist provision and maximum harassment of families in need of either permanent or transient accommodation. The use of extra powers without acting on other provisions of the legislation is a tell-tale sign that little has changed yet in the mindset of council officials to Travellers' accommodation.

Local councils: – the challenge to appreciate the Traveller economy

Home space and work space tend to be one and the same within the Traveller economy. Can local councils come to appreciate that the Traveller economy is based on generating income as opposed to creating jobs and, make provision for home-based work on sites? At the moment councils make it a condition of Travellers tenancy that they do not use their home base for generating income!

Local councils: – the forced break up of culture

I have also begun to see that as in the case of the Eskimos in Canada, the Aboriginals in Australia and the Native Indian tribes in the Amazon basin, the culture of Travellers is under severe pressure. World-wide studies show that when this happens then there is an increase in violence, alcoholism, marriage break up etc. It happened in Dublin when older established communities were broken up and the families transferred to new housing estates. As Michael McDonagh points out, "Travellers are not being allowed to change in a natural way, the way they would have all along, because now more than ever it's a forced change which has a negative effect". He also says "When travel becomes just a dream, a long-delayed dream for the Traveller, despair and its effects set in (illness, break up of the family, aggressiveness and delinquency). The result is a crisis in the society.

Some of the symptoms mentioned above are manifestations of the pressures being put on Travellers from the wider society. For example, Travellers are not used to being forced to live in big numbers and with very different mixes of families as is the case in some of the Official Permanent and Temporary sites, particularly in Dublin, where Councils are following a policy of "isolation" as an answer to the accommodation crisis that local councils have brought on themselves through culpable inaction over the last twenty-five years.

The long shadow of discrimination and social exclusion

The pain of discrimination

> When I sit down and really think about the reality of discrimination, I have a great sense of disbelief at the whole unfairness of it. If you can see unfairness in a situation then it's logical to think that everyone else should be able to see it too.
>
> (Winnie McDonagh)

It's even more painful when you see that most Irish people not only can't see how unfair and unjust it is, but in fact act out the same discriminatory practices in their own lives. It's hard for us as settled people to understand what effects this has especially on young Traveller children growing up, who begin to realise that discrimination is a daily experience that pervades the very fabric of Traveller life and seriously impairs young Travellers from fully participating in society.

I, like my predecessors in this Parish, find the baptism of every Traveller child a very painful experience because everytime I repeat the words, "Josie, the Christian community welcomes you with great joy", I feel very sad knowing that this young Traveller child, is not going to experience this welcome in Irish society today. Josie will soon learn and repeatedly be told in a variety of different ways "sorry, but you're not welcome", to live near our houses, or go to our school, disco, launderette, or pub.

Cathleen McDonagh describes this pain,

> I see the pain of the face of the young person as they try to make sense of the rejection they have experienced. The eyes that hold back the tears of both anger and confusion as they speak of what has happened. The young person who cannot get into the disco, the middle- aged man trying to go for a social drink, the young family with nowhere to stay. I would ask the reader what would you say to a child as they asked you why?

The growth of discrimination

The First Commission on Itinerancy 1963 said "the plight of Travellers has not troubled the public conscience to any degree". This could well have been written in the year 2000. The Irish Bishops stated in 1985 that "The Travellers are the most discriminated against group in Irish society." Ten years later Michael McGreil said that attitudes towards the Traveller community have hardened and his survey led him to conclude that "the picture emerging from the above examination of Irish people's prejudices against the Travellers is one of caste-like apartheid." (*Prejudice in Ireland Revisited 1996*). Irish society has and continues to perpetrate a terrible injustice on the Traveller community. With the recent influx of refugees and asylum-seekers Irish society has shown itself to be very intolerant and racist. This has surprised many people and yet the reality is that racism has been alive and rampant for a long time in Ireland in regard to the Traveller community.

Ridicule – the first stage of discrimination

At every social event I attend, when people find out where I'm working, invariably the funny story, the anecdote or the bad experience is told to me and the generalisation is made that "all Travellers" are like this. The reality is that very few settled people, 1% to be precise, know a Traveller personally, (*CROSSCARE survey 1995*) and yet they have very strong opinions about them based on, what I would term the 'pooled ignorance of the anecdote' or, on what they have learnt from the stereotypical images presented in the media. A recent survey found that while there is a very positive attitude towards Traveller culture and identity, 65% of people are negatively disposed towards Travellers because of their "way of life". (*Citizen Traveller national survey on attitudes to Travellers and minority groups, February 2000*). All the major Traveller organisations in Dublin did an assessment in 1997 which revealed that 20 families out of about 1000 families in the Dublin area were identified as being involved in begging (on the street or door-to-door) and yet it is this minority of Travellers who are responsible for the main bulk of contact with the settled community. There is little desire on the behalf of settled people to see the value in Travellers' lifestyle but nevertheless, there is strength in their dismissal of it. I find this very hurtful.

I often respond in these situations by telling the story of the time I was in Maynooth college with four Travellers who were talking to a group of students about their culture and way of life. On two occasions one student asked Bernadette, a Traveller, to explain why Travellers drink too much. On both occasions she answered him. Later at the coffee break I was present when once again he asked her the same question. Her reply highlighted his ignorance. "Listen", she said, "every morning I drive into my work in the Parish Office in Cook Street. I have to pass down along the quays past the Simon hostel. Almost every morning I have a settled man bang on the window of my car looking for money. He is already drunk. I don't generalise and ask you why do settled people drink so much!" As Cathleen McDonagh points out, 'ridicule' is the first stage of acting out prejudice and these stages are sequential or progressive. I have begun to see that this is true and that all prejudice and racism begin with the funny story.

I worked in Nigeria for five years and many of the Nigerian ways appear "funny" to western culture. Nigerians do things differently to

Westerners. Many of the expatriate population used these "funny" incidents as a way of portraying the Nigerians, whom they regarded as inferior, whereas in reality it was simply a matter of cultural difference. As Delores O'Sullivan points out in her chapter on culture, "It is too easy for a person to believe that their culture is better than some other person's culture. to a person from another culture, their reasons for acting in a certain way can be as logical as our reasons for doing it differently." Travellers have their own cultural traits that settled people might find strange and vice versa. The difference is that in the case of Travellers each relation of such incidents adds to the stereotype and generalisation that prejudice grows on. In regard to this area, we are all personally challenged to look at our attitudes and practices. It is one area where each one of us can practically make a difference.

Health

Accommodation and Health

It is an extraordinary indictment of Ireland at the start of the 21st Century that it has 1,250 families living on the side of the road without toilets, water, electricity, refuse collection etc., all of which most members of the settled community take for granted. Approximately 50% of these 6,000people living on the side of the road are under the age of fifteen. The Pavee Point Womens Primary Health Care Project highlighted the fact that "Travellers only now reach the life expectancy of the settled population in the nineteen forties and the infant mortality in the Traveller population is three times the national average." They point out that the poor living conditions mean that Travellers suffer from more diseases and are less likely to look after their health as they have difficulty attending hospitals or making doctor appointments. They point out that Traveller sites are often located beside dumps, graveyards or main roads which increases the risk of transmitting disease.

Travellers making the decisions that shape their lives

The success of the Primary Health Care for Travellers Project developed by Pavee point lies in its provision of a model of good practice for the rest of the country. The progress in the new developments are encouraging, but it will take time for them to impact on Traveller health. It is therefore very disturbing to read that "To date only six of the eight health boards have set up a Traveller Health Unit and some of those established have not followed the guidelines in *The Report of the Task Force on the Travelling Community 1995*". This is literally a matter of life or death for many Travellers and it highlights the grave need for positive discrimination to bring about real "equality of condition" for Travellers in Irish society. As it is settled people in positions of power who are making the decisions in regard to Travellers healthcare, Travellers are being denied their basic human right of being able to participate in shaping the decisions that affect their lives

Education

A monocultural system resisting change?

Ireland has prided itself on its education system which it sees as one of the foundation stones of the success of the present day economy. Nevertheless, this education system has been and continues to be monocultural and makes little attempt to be inclusive of other cultures living within our state. As Mairin Kenny states "Our society is increasingly intent on controlling diversity, an urge forcefully expressed in our continued exclusion of Travellers and in our noisy noxious attempts to close our doors to immigrants."

The effects of monoculturalism: loss of identity

The Traveller child does not benefit from education in the way their settled peers do. While most Traveller children attend primary school very few transfer to second level. The figures showing that there are only 961 Traveller children in post primary education in 1999 are startling. This is easily understood when one realises that the curriculum does not recognise or value Traveller culture. In many cases Travellers have to hide their identity to continue in the system and parents are very afraid that the current monocultural system damages their child's identity. As one parent describes,

> Young ones going to secondary school change into something they're not. They're acting like country people. They're dressing like country people.

They don't like jewellery no more. They don't like being a Traveller. They're trying to be something that they're not. The point I'm making is - the way you go in is the way you should come out with plenty of education but still proud to be a Traveller.

Michael McDonagh makes the same point when he writes: "Once they have accepted that being a Traveller is something to be ashamed of, the next step is to try to change, to become a settled person". Michael McGreil talks of Travellers being 'deradicalised' i.e. cut off from their roots, because they do not have their culture recognised in our educational material. Travellers are being cut off from their roots.

Intercultural education – the need for anti-racist proofing

One day a young Traveller boy rushed into his mother and said "Mammy I was at school today!". The mother replied "I know you were in school today, why are you telling me?" The boy explained "Today the teacher brought in a picture of a caravan"

The story may be simple but the questions it raises about our educational policy, practice and our curriculum cut to the heart of the matter. The reality is that Traveller children do not find themselves at home in a homogenous and monocultural curriculum and system. If we are serious about creating true equality of condition in regard to education, then "resources and materials are needed to implement an intercultural, anti-racist curriculum" and in order to achieve this " the content of texts should be monitored to avoid ethnocentric and racist interpretation". The focus of the curriculum should not rest on the exotic customs of Travellers which reinforce negative stereotypes, but on the broader equality and human rights issues. (*The Report of the Task Force on the Travelling People 1995*). Equality proofing is the process of implementing equality objectives built into a variety of social and economic policies. Equality proofing of the entire curriculum and of all educational policy must take place if an intercultural system of education, which embraces the richness of cultural diversity, is to be established. (*Equality Proofing Administrative Procedures 1998*)

Equality of condition in the education system

Equality of condition demands a revision of our current programmes, policies and philosophies of education in developing an integrated, holistic and multi-cultural system of education, which seeks to actively engage all people irrespective of gender, minority-status etc., in meaningful life-long learning. (*Sheehan 2000*) Almost half of the recommendations of (*The Report of the Task Force for the Travelling People 1995*) is concerned with education. One of the reasons for the lack of progress in implementing the recommendations at second-level is the number of different sections in the Department of Education and the lack of co-ordination between them. The *Task Force* recommended, (as did the *Department of Education Working Group 1992* and the I*NTO Report 1992*) the establishment of a Traveller Education Service. It is regrettable that the Department of Education and Science has not acted on this recommendation thus ensuring that "equality of condition" for Traveller children is further postponed.

In regard to education, for example, we are challenged to review not only our present policies surrounding this very contentious issue but our very philosophy of education. Failure to recognise, affirm and value Traveller culture in the education system is to do a violence to every Traveller child who enters the classroom. This is one of the biggest challenges facing our educators and policy makers.

The social economy

Travellers and the 'informal' economy

Experts from every field of professionalism, both at home and abroad, are praising and affirming values of self-employment, enterprise, recycling and apprenticeship. Travellers have worked in accordance with these values in the past and continue to do so now. Nevertheless, they are criticised and despised precisely because they value these approaches to the economy that are central to their way of life. This is a curious paradox. Is this because, as Michael McDonagh says,

> Traveller entire economy is informal but it is true to say that most settled people view it negatively? I think this is because many settled people see Travellers as sort of second-class citizens because the perception is that they are involved with the "black " or "informal" economy which settled people see as illegal.

Broadening our concept of work

The challenge posed to members of the settled community is to appreciate and value the qualities of enterprise and initiative that are present in the Traveller community. These qualities which are now coming to be recognised as the development of the social economy and of a wider understanding of work are seen by many as a way forward for the Irish and European economy. *The European Commission White Paper 'Growth, Competitiveness, Employment' 1993)* emphasised the importance of the social economy and stressed the need for "a wider concept of work, incorporating all forms of paid or partially paid work within a common framework comprising the social economy, intermediate employment enterprises and the informal economy".

Faith and the Traveller community

Spirituality

The power of blessings

For Travellers God is close. Their spirituality is one that sees and discovers God in everyday events and is very much rooted in the Celtic tradition. Travellers call on a God whom they believe hears their prayers and will respond. God is to be found especially in blessings which are seen as the touch of God in a Traveller's life. Travellers will ask for God's blessing for themselves and others. My only childhood memory of Travellers is of them coming to the door and saying a prayer of blessing when my mother gave them a cup of tea and some old clothes. I still feel moved as I remember a most touching blessing an old Traveller woman gave me at her bedside a few days before she died. Travellers use these blessings in a very natural way when looking at a young child or when asking God to bless a pregnant mother and her new born baby or a sick relative or a new van or caravan. As Cathleen McDonagh said "there is within us the need for God's protection in this life; we seek the blessing of God all through life for everything that is connected to our lives."

The journey of faith

Traveller faith flows naturally into and out of all aspects of everyday

life. It is as natural for a Traveller, male for female, young or old, to go on pilgrimage to Croagh Patrick, Knock, Lourdes, a holy well or to a holy person as it is for them to breathe the air around them. "Here and there, on the road, there are places where the presence of God is sensed more powerfully. Travellers all know these holy places and holy wells" (Colm Kilcoyne).

Pilgrimages are a very important expression of a Traveller's prayer. They are physical, ritual prayers where the journey is the prayer which they undertake for the benefit of another, just as Margaret Lawrence so poignantly climbed the Reek for her young niece and in the pilgrimage gave her life. Cathleen McDonagh says of pilgrimages that, "At the centre of these practices is the belief in a God who is accessible and present within people's existence. If you can see life as a journey then you will see God walks with us on this life journey."

Mourning the dead

I have been deeply moved and humbled by the strength and resilience of so many Traveller families who are forced to live in appalling conditions and at the same time have to cope with so many tragedies. Most of the funerals I have had to lead have been of people who have died long before their time. So many of the deaths arise out of the living conditions and the social exclusion which most Travellers live with on a daily basis. I have been enriched by the open, natural grieving process where parents and children, husbands and wives openly cry and talk to their dead relative in the mortuary. They pour out their grief like Hannah in the Book of Samuel who said, when the priest Eli accused her of being drunk, "I have been praying here out of my great anguish and grief". I have witnessed this kind of prayer too often as mothers and fathers grieved the deaths of so many young children in a community whose infant mortality rate is three times the national average. Traveller prayer is very biblical. It is in the tradition of lamentation for what could have been and is not.

One of the images that is strongest in my mind is that of families, huge extended families gathered in celebration at a baptism, wedding in solidarity and support at a hospital bed as a relative struggled for life, or in mourning at the burial. In Anne O Brien's article we got a glimpse of the rich customs and traditions Travellers have around death and grieving with a healthy and open mourning of the dead-which we as settled people may have lost from our Irish tradition. To make these customs more readily available and as a help to service providers (e.g. priests, nurses undertakers, teachers, guards etc.) to Travellers, we in the coming year will be publishing a book about Travellers' experience of death and grief. This arose out of a research project, engaged in by a group of Travellers, about their traditions in this area.

Our response in the Parish to creating equality of condition

The work of the Parish of the Travelling People

Nurturing faith

We in the Parish of the Travelling People endeavour to resource a faith that is informed by a people with a nomadic identity and a long rich oral tradition . We believe that any discussion of Traveller culture and nomadism has to include their very strong faith beliefs and rich religious traditions. Traveller culture influences the expressions and practices of faith. It is a dynamic, not static, entity and so the faith expressions of Travellers are changing. As Winnie McDonagh said, "Even though many young Travellers have distanced themselves from the organised Church (because of the scandals) they still believe in prayer, Our Blessed Lady, the mercy of God, the saints they haven't lost faith in God"

Traveller and Settled working in solidarity

We in the Parish of the Travelling People have come to recognise the need to work in partnership with Travellers to help change structures and attitudes in society as a whole. We try to live with the tension of providing a pastoral service to all the Travellers in the Dublin Diocese, while at the same time working hard to resource, in particular, local parishes and the Irish Church, nationally. We find it difficult to understand why Travellers are challenged on a daily basis to give reasons why they should be allowed to celebrate their own culture and to exist. We are very committed to having what Thomas McCann describes as "a partnership approach of settled and Traveller working together, as equals, with a shared goal in mind". Pope John Paul 11 said, "in a sense, respect for minorities is to be considered the touchstone of social harmony and the index of the civic maturity achieved by a country and its institutions". (*To Build Peace, Respect Minorities, 1989*) In offering culturally-appropriate services to Travellers, this Parish stands in solidarity and partnership with Travellers who are excluded in so many ways by Irish society and its administrative structures.

Justice and helping to build up right relationships based on respect for human dignity and the common good within the community are key concerns for the Parish which serves a people who are forced by the accommodation policy of local councils to live on the edge of society. Justice means challenging the settled faith community about its role in this exclusion and oppression that leaves Travellers witnessing to the Kingdom in isolated sites on the margins of society.

Networking with Traveller organisations

The Parish is strongly committed to working in partnership and networking with other organisations and individuals working with Travellers. In striving to create a more just society where Travellers are recognised and accepted as full and equal citizens, the need to work in collaboration with other Traveller organisations has grown. Networking with other Traveller organisations such as The Irish Traveller Movement, Pavee Point and The National Traveller Womens Forum and with local Traveller support groups developed over the years to try and bring about affective change and justice-making structures at statutory, relational and social levels. The Citizen Traveller Campaign is a good example of the effectiveness of networking in lobbying the Government for money to provide a positive media campaign to promote Travellers as an ethnic group.

Local Parishes: building relationships between Traveller and settled

We are very aware that we have a privileged entry point into the life of the two hundred local parishes in the Diocese of Dublin. Therefore part of our strategy is to encourage and resource Church leaders and local parish teams to actively include Travellers in the lives of their local parishes as equal and as full members. We see that the key factor in increasing the participation of Travellers in society, especially at local parish level, is the building up of relationships. *The Report of the Task Force on the Travelling Community 1995* devoted its first chapter to the primacy of relationships between the Traveller and settled communities. It states that,

> The improvement of relationships between the Traveller and 'Settled' communities through the development of mutual understanding and respect requires an adjustment in attitudes towards one another and an acceptance of the other's culture. The Task Force believes that church groups have a significant role to play in this area, particularly in the improvement of relations between 'Settled' and Traveller populations.

From our experience of pilot projects we have learnt that the best way to build up relationships is through action-based projects or events of common interest like an exhibition, sale of work, pilgrimage or mass for the dead in November. In this way both groups participate as equals, because as the Citizen Traveller survey concludes "People with a favourable attitude towards Travellers are much more likely than average to have socialised with them, to have worked with them or to have had Travellers do some odd jobs on their behalf". (*Citizen Traveller national survey on attitudes to Travellers and minority groups, February 2000*)

Conclusion: hopes for a better future

I hope that:

> this book may be another little step in helping to create a society in which Travellers are recognised and acknowledged as full and equal citizens of Ireland

> Traveller culture and way of life will come to be understood, valued and appreciated in the minds and hearts of all Irish citizens

> Travellers will really be listened to and given their fundamental human right of being able to participate in shaping the decisions that affect their lives

> the will to solve the accommodation problem will be there on the part of local councils and the people of Ireland, so that the scandal of the appalling conditions in which Travellers have been

forced to live in for so many years will finally, over the next five years, be resolved

Traveller culture will be given its rightful place in the curriculum of our schools, especially in second level education

"equality of condition" so necessary for Travellers in gaining access to education and proper health-care etc. would become a priority in government policy, and that the Equal Status Legislation will make a real difference in the lives of Travellers.

In particular I hope that through the work of the Traveller organisations and support groups and especially through the endeavours of the Citizen Traveller Campaign that there will be a gradual change in attitudes that is so necessary if Travellers are to take their full and rightful place in Irish society and if the two communities of Traveller and settled are to come to know, appreciate and value each other.

"We cannot change the past be we can create a better future." These words were spoken by President McAleese (in the conclusion of her Christmas address to the Oireachtas) who, in the preface of this book, underlined how we might create this better future by releasing the full potential and talents of Travellers and other ethnic groups through understanding , respecting, cherishing and embracing the richness that diversity brings. We have never been good at accepting difference in Ireland. Travellers are such a small group (less than 1.0% of the population) that we have comfortably ignored them. However, the influx of refugees and asylum seekers is forcing us to look at the underlying attitudes of prejudice and racism that are not far below the surface. We are now being challenged, for the first time, to work to create an intercultural society that respects Travellers and other minority groups and to,

> Overcome the myths, prejudices and labelling that have been handed down as unshakeable truths, to listen and to slowly grow in understanding, to discover the awesome power that can be harnessed when different traditions embrace each other widely and warmly.
>
> (President Mary McAleese)

This challenge to create a better future for Travellers and settled in Ireland can be seen in the poignant words of Seamus Heaney in his poem "Cure at Troy":

So hope for a great sea-change
On the far side of revenge.
Believe that a farther shore
Is reachable from here.
Believe in miracles
And cures and healing wells.

Travellers' appeal for Romanian children

On two occasions (1996 and 1998) Travellers and settled, working in partnership, drove four vans carrying thousands of pounds of much needed supplies, medical equipment and toys to a Romanian orphanage at Vidra. These supplies were made or donated by Travellers from all over Ireland

Appendix 1

Glossary

Cant

The Traveller language is called Gammon or Cant. In academic circles it is referred to as Shelta. Research into the Traveller language has interpreted the manner in which the language has developed as a product of a nomadic group, the members of which were only in intermittent contact with each other. In this way the vocabulary is well developed while the grammar is borrowed from the majority 'Settled' community. The development of a grammar requires a fixed stable community.

Country person

Travellers use this term when referring to a settled person.

Culture

Definitions of culture encompass reference to those things which are held in common by a society or group e.g. worldview, lifestyle, beliefs, values, customs, traditions, patterns of thought and behaviour, organisation of relationships, roles. The single most important thing about culture is that it is learned.

Cultural Diversity

At its most basic, cultural diversity simply refers to the reality of cultural difference. At another level, however, it reflects a concern to promote openness and tolerance within the context of an increasingly multi-cultural world.

Discrimination

Discrimination is prejudice in action. It occurs when a person or group is treated differently or less favourably than others, often on the basis of race or colour. Discriminatory action can be carried out by individuals or by groups and institutions. (See also Prejudice)

Ethnic Group

A group of people who share a collective identity based on a common history. They possess their own culture, customs, norms, beliefs and traditions. They may also share language, geographical origin, ancestors, literature, religion and the experience of being oppressed. Ethnic groups may be a majority or minority group within a larger community. Boundaries between members and non-members are maintained.

Ethnocentrism

Opinions or beliefs which glorify one's own culture or nationality, often at the expense of others. Can be accompanied by a dislike of or contempt for other groups/cultures.

Gammon

See Cant

Nomadism

A way of life based on earning a livelihood in a manner which requires moving the place of one's home, at least periodically. The economics of nomadism arise from and affect social organisation and, most importantly, cultural identity.

> Whereas a sedentary person remains sedentary, even when travelling, the Traveller is a nomad, even when he does not travel. Immobilised, he remains a Traveller
>
> (*Liégeois, Gypsies and Travellers 1987*)

Prejudice

An opinion or belief about something or someone which is formed without reasonable knowledge or experience. Prejudice is usually negative. Racial prejudice may be directed towards a group as a whole or towards individuals because of their membership of that group and differs from discrimination in that it does not necessarily involve action.

Race

Is a social construct rather than a biological phenomenon based on dividing up the single human race on the basis of biological or cultural differences and creating hierarchies on the basis of this difference. It came into usage in the English language during the 16th century, a major period of colonisation to justify the destruction and domination of other cultures by claiming that they were inferior, savage, uncivilised or even sub-human. Irish people were also categorised in this way.

> As a way of categorising people race is based upon a delusion because popular ideas about racial classification lack scientific validity and are moulded by political pressures rather than by the evidence from biology.
>
> Banton M. and Harwood J.

Racism

A belief that cultural traits and capacities are racially determined. It justifies and acts upon the assumption that some races are naturally superior or inferior.

Racism is an oppression based on power relations between groups built on the use and abuse of skin colour, cultural difference or imagined physical difference.

> Any theory which involves the claim that racial or ethnic groups are inherently superior or inferior, thus implying that some would be entitled to dominate or eliminate others, presumed to be inferior, or which bases value judgements on racial differentiation, has no scientific foundation and is contrary to the moral and ethical principles of humanity.
>
> UNESCO 1978

Institutional racism

Is where the activities, practices, policies or laws of an institution lead, intentionally or unintentionally, to less favourable outcomes for minority ethnic groups.

Sedentarism

A lifestyle which involves staying in one place giving rise to specific forms of economic and social organisation as well as cultural identity

Stereotyping

Originally referred to metal plates, which were used in printing to fix an image. Hence the understanding of stereotype as a "fixed - image" attitude towards individuals or groups irrespective of their differences. This form of generalisation can give rise to a tendency to think or act in rigid and repetitive ways

Sub-culture

A group, some of whose values, attitudes, beliefs etc. differ to a greater or lesser extent from those of the dominant culture.

Vessels

The term Travellers use when referring to cutlery etc.

Visiting Teacher

The purpose of the visiting teacher service is to support and advise families in placing their children in school oftentimes by approaching schools directly on the behalf of parents. The service keeps the families informed of developments in schools and keeps schools informed of relevant home background information and attempts to bridge the gap between the culture of the home and the culture of the school.

Most of the definitions are taken from the *Pavee Pack*, a resource pack for teachers of the C.S.P.E. programme in post-primary schools.

Appendix 2

History of Legislation and other Milestones

1963   Commission on Itinerancy
        Recommended the assimilation of Travellers into the settled community.

1983   Report of the Travelling People Review Body
        Promoted the integration of Travellers into mainstream society without adequately supporting and promoting their cultural identity.

1988   Housing Act
        Provides the first statutory recognition of Traveller specific accommodation.

1991   Prohibition of Incitement to Hatred Act
        Prohibits incitement to hatred on the ground of race, colour, religion, ethnic or national origin, membership of the Traveller community and sexual orientation. No case has been successfully brought under this act.

1992   Housing (Miscellaneous Provisions) Act
        Section 10 of this act empowers local authorities to remove Travellers, who are camped unofficially, to an official site anywhere within a five mile radius of where they are.

1993   Roads Act
        Relevant to Traveller accommodation but makes very little direct mention of the special needs of the Traveller Community. The Act empowers Local Authorities and Gardai to remove temporary dwellings in certain circumstances.

1994   Shaping A Healthier Future: A Strategy for Effective Health-Care in the 1990s: Report by the Department of Health
        Contained a section on Traveller Health and pledged to

implement a special programme to address the particular health needs of the Traveller Community.

1995   White Paper on Education: 'Charting our Education Future'
Calls for full participation in school life by Traveller Children by means of integration while at the same time respecting Traveller culture.

1995   Casual Trading Act
This Act requires market traders to apply to each local authority for a casual licence for any market in their area. This resulted in increased costs for engagement in market trading. Previously only one licence was required for the whole country.

1995   Developing a Policy for Women's Health
This report analyses morbidity and mortality rates and trends for women in Ireland. It identified categories of women at risk within Irish society, and included Traveller women.

1995   Report of the Task Force on the Travelling Community
This makes numerous recommendations covering all aspects of Traveller life and Government policy relating to Travellers and acknowledges the distinct culture and identity of the Traveller community.

1997   Plan for Women's Health
Pavee Point commissioned a researcher to prepare a response to The Report on Traveller Women's Health. This plan acknowledged that Traveller women have a role in increasing the uptake of health services, by encouraging their peers to avail of these services.

1997   Control of Horses Act
Places restriction on the ownership of horses.

1998   Housing (Traveller Accommodation) Act
Obliges local authorities to meet the current and projected needs of the Traveller Community. Sections of the Act give increased powers of eviction to Local Authorities.

1999   Employment Equality Act
This Act outlaws discrimination in the employment field on

several grounds including membership of the Traveller community

1999   Equality Authority Established
This body was established with responsibility for the implementation of the Employment Equality Act and the forthcoming Equal Status Legislation.

2000   Equal Status Act
This covers the issue of discrimination in the provision of services.

Appendix 3

The Task Force Recommendations

Adopting a Partnership Approach

The Report of the Task Force on the Travelling Community 1995 produced its report in July 1995. It represented a partnership of Travellers and settled people, voluntary organisations, Government Departments and elected representatives. It is a most comprehensive examination of the situation of the Traveller community and contains significant and convincing proposals for changing the negative issues that Travellers face in Ireland today.

The Report has been widely welcomed by Travellers and Traveller organisations. It presents the possibility of a new future for Travellers. The key challenge now is to ensure the full implementation of the Task Force recommendations.

The Report places a great emphasis on the participation of Travellers and Traveller organisations in areas of decision making that affect the Traveller community. The Report also highlights the range of different roles played by Traveller organisations.

Recognition of the distinct culture and identity of the Traveller community

What sets this Report apart from similar reports made in 1983 and 1963 is its early acknowledgement of the distinct culture and identity of Travellers. A chapter is devoted to examining this topic and concludes by stating that *"the distinct culture and identity of the Traveller community need to be recognised and taken into account"*.

The Creation of National Structures to Implement Recommendations in the following areas,

• Accommodation

At national level, the report recommended the creation of a Traveller

Accommodation Agency with the resources and powers to support and monitor annual programmes of Traveller accommodation provision, implemented by Local Authorities. *The National Travellers' Accommodation Consultative Committee* was established in December 1996. The work of the committee to date has included making inputs into *"The Guidelines for Permanent Accommodation, Caravan Parks, Transient Sites"*, *"The Housing (Traveller Accommodation) Act 1998"*, *"Accommodation Options"* and *"The Management and Maintenance of Traveller Accommodation"*. Finally they monitor accommodation provision for Travellers on a national scale.

In regard to Traveller specific accommodation the Report recommends a combination of standard housing, group housing, permanent halting sites and transient halting sites be provided for Travellers. It is estimated in 1995, that 3,100 units of accommodation were required to deal with the existing backlog in the provision of accommodation with 1,100 families on the side of the road. The Report recommends that temporary sites should be phased out by the year 2000 with existing temporary sites upgraded where appropriate to the standard of permanent or transient sites. Since then however, only 123 units of accommodation have been provided and the number of Travellers on temporary sites and on the roadside has increased.

• **Education**

It is worth noting that almost half of the recommendations of *The Report of the Task Force on the Travelling Community 1995* are dedicated to the subject of education provision for Travellers. The report recognises that one of the main reasons for the failure of Travellers to make substantial progress in second-level education is the lack of a co-ordinated approach to Traveller education and the division of responsibility for Traveller education provision between a number of different sections in the Department of Education. The Report recommends the setting up of a Traveller Education Service made up of a Traveller Education Unit and an Advisory Committee at national level which would have overall responsibility for the development of Traveller education and for the co-ordination of activities in the various sections of the Department dealing with the education needs of Travellers. Apart from the establishment of an Advisory Committee on Traveller Education in 1998, The Department of Education and Science has failed to act on these recommendations.

The approach in education recommended by the Task Force is one of *integration* based on an *intercultural curriculum*. Such a curriculum would be based on a number of principles including respect for all cultures, information about minority groups, a focus on equality and human rights issues and an active avoidance of racist interpretations in text.

Special pre-schools for Traveller children were identified as having a very positive impact on Travellers' experience of education. The report highlights the need for a national policy of pre-school education with a standard programme to be developed by the Department of Education. An immediate increase to thirty-nine teachers in the highly commended Visiting Teacher Service is also recommended in the report, with an extension of their mandate to cover both primary and second- level schooling. Progress has been made with the number of Visiting Teachers being increased to 30 in 1999.

• Health

The Report recommends the creation of a Traveller Health Advisory Committee within the Department of Health to develop policies to improve the health status of Travellers and to ensure co-ordination and liaison in the implementation of national strategies. *The Traveller Health Advisory Committee* was established in November 1998. Since then it has focused its attention on the development of a National Traveller Health Strategy which should be available in early 2000 and which will inform the future direction in Traveller health.

Traveller-specific health services are recommended to improve Travellers' access to mainstream services. Primary health-care is stressed and peer-led services (which involve the employment of Travellers to provide a service within their own community) are recommended in this area. The Report mentions, in particular, The Eastern Health Board/Pavee Point Primary Health Care programme and replication of this programme is recommended. In-service training on the *"circumstances, culture of, and discrimination practised against Travellers"*, is also recommended for all health professionals.

At a local level it was suggested that each local authority would have a Traveller Accommodation Committee *"representing a partnership based on fair representation on the principle of equality, of local authority councillors, Travellers and Traveller organisations"*. This committee would assist in the development and implementation of the accommodation programme and of Traveller tenant participation strategies.

At a regional level it was recommended that each Health Board would set up a Traveller Health Unit. This would ensure that a prominence is given to Traveller health issues and that targets are set and monitored in this area.

•Discrimination

The issue of discrimination is an underlying theme throughout the Task Force Report. As such, it is appropriate that the *Task Force* was set up by the Government Department which has responsibility for Equal Status Legislation. The report highlights the importance of this legislation and recommended that it would

> Identify that neither direct nor indirect discrimination against Travellers could be justified on the grounds of potential financial disadvantage to the provider

and that it would

> Prohibit...
>> Policies and procedures that discriminate against Travellers culture and identity;
>> The exclusion of Travellers, just because they are Travellers, from the normal benefit of goods, services and facilities;
>> The segregation of Travellers in the general provision of goods, services and facilities unless this is for reason of positive action.

•Special needs

Finally, the report also identifies that Travellers are not a homogeneous group. Separate sections deal with the particular situation and needs of Traveller women and Travellers with special needs i.e. Travellers with a disability. The Report recommended that

> In implementing each of the recommendations addressed in this report the

gender dimension should be examined to ascertain how policies and practices in each area contribute to or block progress for Traveller women.

The Committee to monitor and co-ordinate the Implementation of the Recommendations of the Task Force.

This committee, established in 1998, focuses on the Traveller Economy and the Human Rights Commission and in addition looks at the progress achieved on all the Task Force Recommendations. It is hoped that a progress report will be published towards the end of 2000.

Representation on the National Traveller Committees

The Irish Traveller Movement co-operates with the National Traveller Women's Forum and Pavee Point in relation to representing Traveller interests on all the National Traveller Committees. Working-group structures within the organisations are used to give feedback and obtain input into the work of these committees. In addition distinct meetings are arranged to ensure that there is a linkage between the members of the organisations and the work of the committees.

Appendix 4

Travellers and Education: Statistics

Traveller children in primary schools

1963	114
1988	4000
1999	5000

Traveller children in post primary schools

1992	100
1998	800
1999	961

Number of Traveller children in post primary October 1999 and distribution by year

1st year:	478
2nd year:	266
3rd year:	116
4th year:	31
5th year:	51
6th year:	19
P.L.C.	1
TOTAL	961

Travellers in third level

1997	4

Resource teachers for Traveller children in primary schools

1992	150
1999	400

Visiting teachers for Traveller children (cf. note next page)

1980	1
1982	4
1992	9
1995	12
1997	20
2000	30

Special schools for Travellers – 1998

Pre- Schools	52
Special Primary Schools	2
Post Primary Schools with teaching hours	130
Junior Education Centres	8 (130 students)
Senior Training Centres	28 (650 students)

Schools with special classes for Traveller children

(Correction of misleading Task Force figures in 1995)

Statistics on Traveller participation in education provision can be unreliable, as there is no administrative mechanism to name pupils according to their ethnic identity. One source of statistics is the Special Education Section of The Department of Education and Science. This section would, through their resources programme for Travellers, record the number of Travellers in receipt of learning/resource support in primary schools. This support which began in the 1970's was termed "special classes" and continued to be known by this name for administrative purposes up until 1996 in the Department's statistics of Travellers in special classes. In practice some schools availed of the "special teacher" but never established special classes. In a Department of Education survey in 1988, 30% of Travellers were recorded as being in special classes, i.e. approximately 700 Traveller children in fifty special classes. The *Report of the Task Force on the Traveller Community 1995* depended on quoted Special Education Statistics referring to the 200 "special teachers" as "special classes". At the time of the publication of the *Task Force report,* I estimate there were approximately 12 special classes as such.

(All the above statistics and comment are from Maugie Francis, The National Education Officer for Traveller Education, December, 1999).

The visiting teacher service for Travellers

To respond to the educational needs of Traveller children, The Department of Education initiated a pilot project in Galway in 1980, whereby a visiting teacher was appointed to make and maintain contact with Traveller families in the Galway area in promoting greater participation of Traveller children in school. The project was established on a permanent basis in 1982 with a further four visiting teachers appointed for Dublin, Cork and Limerick. Another expansion of the service took place in 1992 to cover Kerry, Wexford and the expanding Traveller population in Dublin, bringing the total number of teachers to nine. In response to the recommendations of the *The Report of the Task Force on the Travelling Community 1995* this number was increased to 30 in 1999.

The Visiting Teachers service supports and advises Traveller families in placing their children in school oftentimes by approaching schools directly on behalf of parents. The service keeps the families informed of developments in schools and more importantly keeps schools informed of relevant home background information. The service attempts to bridge the gap between the culture of the home and the culture of the school. The Visiting Teacher Service works closely with existing statutory and voluntary services to provide the maximum back-up support to families and their school-going children. The service also works closely with the National Education Officer for Travellers who was first appointed by the Department of Education in 1992. It is the responsibility of the National Education Officer to coordinate and develop policy and practice in relation to Traveller Education.

Appendix 5

Traveller Accommodation: Statistics

There are approximately 5,000 Traveller families or an estimated 28,000 Travellers in Ireland (about 1000 Travellers live in Northern Ireland). Travellers constitute less than 1% of the national population. 50% of all Travellers live in four counties with, 23% in Dublin, 11% in Galway, 8% in Cork and 7% in Limerick. Almost half of the Traveller population is under the age of 15. It is estimated that there is a 4% annual increase in the number of Travellers. It is also estimated that 15,000 Irish Travellers live in Britain with a further 10,000 Travellers of Irish descent living in the Unites States of America.

The following pages contain accommodation statistics provided by the Department of the Environment for November 1999.

Travellers live in:

1. Local authority standard houses

2. Local authority Traveller specific group housing schemes

3. Private houses or houses provided by voluntary bodies with local authority assistance.

4. Local authority Traveller specific halting sites (permanent and temporary)

5. On the roadside (indigenous or transient): see Pat Brady p.110 and Frank Murphy p.188

6. Other private accommodation

Traveller families in (1) Local authority or local authority assisted accommodation, (2) on the roadside, or (3) other private accommodation Position at November 1999	ACCOMMODATED			
	Standard local authority housing	Local authority group housing	Private houses assisted by local authority	Priovided by voluntary bodies with L.A assistance
Carlow	17	4	2	1
Cavan	26	0	0	0
Clare	32	10	9	1
Cork (City)	116	0	1	0
Cork (County)	84	16	4	6
Donegal	61	0	0	0
Dublin (City)	43	109	2	0
Dun Laoire/Rathdown	28	24	0	0
Fingal	23	13	0	0
Galway (City)	113	22	1	0
Galway (County)	184	31	7	3
Kerry	181	2	1	0
Kildare	3	0	2	0
Kilkenny	23	3	8	3
Laois	23	1	0	3
Leitrim	2	0	1	0
Limerick (City)	13	10	1	0
LImerick (County)	95	11	29	0
Longford	124	0	2	0
Louth	92	18	16	0
Mayo	90	3	2	0
Meath	54	34	0	4
Monaghan	49	0	0	0
Offaly	51	0	3	1
Roscommon	14	2	0	0
Sligo	19	1	0	0
South Dublin	77	19	18	0
Tipperary (N.R.)	62	0	2	1
Tipperary (S.R.)	36	6	4	0
Waterford (City)	63	0	0	1
Waterford (County)	10	4	0	0
Westmeath	47	0	0	0
Wexford	75	13	11	1
Wicklow	43	0	2	1
TOTALS	1973	356	128	26

Local authority halting sites	Total accommodated by L.A. or with L.A. assistance	ON THE ROAD		TOTAL	
		Indigenous	Transient	Accommodated by or with L.A. assistance & on the roadside	Estimated no. of families in other private accommodation
6	30	30	0	60	15
18	44	5	0	49	0
18	70	37	0	107	3
63	180	12	4	196	5
13	123	28	17	168	55
20	81	35	0	116	3
141	295	95	18	408	3
21	73	23	0	96	0
138	174	83	12	269	0
31	167	26	0	193	28
24	249	80	4	333	0
25	209	13	3	225	2
25	30	15	23	68	7
16	53	8	4	65	2
23	50	15	0	65	1
21	24	0	0	24	0
31	55	7	4	66	1
29	164	53	3	220	4
14	140	6	12	158	6
20	146	11	0	157	25
8	103	56	1	160	7
42	134	8	4	146	5
7	56	0	1	57	9
23	78	56	22	156	8
22	38	9	0	47	0
16	36	12	11	59	0
160	274	90	0	364	2
12	77	29	7	113	0
18	64	21	4	89	5
15	79	8	6	93	32
11	25	1	11	37	0
30	77	11	0	88	64
20	120	110	0	230	23
19	65	26	17	108	0
1100	3583	1019	188	4790	315

Appendix 6
Bibliography

General Reading

Acker, S. (1995) Carry on Caring: the work of women teachers, *British Journal of Sociology of Education*, Vol. 16, No. 1, pp. 21-36

Bagley, C.A. (1992) *In-service provision and teacher resistance to whole-school change* in Gill, D., Mayor, B., & Blair, M. Racism and Education, Structures and Strategies. Sage: London.

Barry, J. & Daly, L. (1998) *The Travellers Health Study*. The Health Board: Dublin.

Binchy, A. (1994) Travellers' Language: A Sociolinguistic Perspective in M.McCann, S.O Siochain and J. Ruane (eds) *Irish Travellers: Culture and Ethnicity* Institute of Irish Studies: Belfast.

Clancy, P. (ed.) (1999) *Celtic Threads*, Veritas Publications: Dublin.

Dunne, M. C. (1998) *Rituals Hove A Place In The Grieving Process of Minority Ethnic Groups*. Unpublished thesis.

Gmelch, G. (1977) *Tinkers and Travellers: The Urbanisation of an Itinerant People*. Cummings: California.

Gmelch, Sharon. (1979) *Tinkers and Travellers: Ireland's Nomads* (Second edition) O'Brien Press: Dublin.

Harding, M (ed.) (1999). *The Road Around the World*, Tullamore Travellers Movement

Kenny, M. (1997) Response to Keynote address, *Glocklai*, Vol. 2, No. 6, pp. 11-13.

Kenny, M (1997) *The Routes of Resistance: Travellers and Second Level Schooling*. Ashgate: Aldershot.

Liégeois, J-P. (1987), *Gypsies and Travellers*, Dossiers for the Intercultural Training of Teachers, Council of Europe Press: Strasbourg.

Mac Laughlin, J. (1995) *Travellers and Ireland: Whose Country,*

Whose History? Undercurrent Series (ed: F. O'Toole),Cork University Press: Cork.

Mc Cann, M. O Siochain, S. and Ruane, J. (eds). (1994) *Irish Travellers: Culture and Ethnicity* Institute of Irish Studies: Belfast

McCarthy, P. (1994) The Sub-culture of Poverty Reconsidered in M. McCann, S. O Siochain and J. Ruane (eds) *Irish Travellers: Culture and Ethnicity* Institute of Irish Studies: Belfast.

McGreil, M. (1997) *Prejudice in Ireland Revisited.* St. Patricks College: Maynooth.

McVeigh, R & Binchy, A. (1998) *Travellers, Refugees & Racism in Tallaght.* West Tallaght Resource Centre: Dublin

Melzak, S. (1995) Cited in workshop report on 'emotional support for Refugee children' in Kenny, M. *Educational Provision for Traveller and Refugee Children: Promoting Achievement Seminar report.* (unpublished) Council of Europe: Strasbourg.

Ni Shuinear, S. (1994) Irish Travellers, Ethnicity and the Origins Question in M.McCann, S.O Siochain and J. Ruane (eds) *Irish Travellers: Culture and Ethnicity* Institute of Irish Studies: Belfast.

O'Reilly, M. (1993), *With Travellers: A Handbook for Teachers,* Blackrock Teachers Centre, Dublin.

Reiss, C. (1975) *The Education of Travelling Children.* Macmillan: London.

Sheehan, E (2000) assignment on the theme of 'equality in education' (unpublished) Maynooth.

Short, G. & Carrington, B. (1992) *Towards an anti-racist initiative in the all-white primary school: a case study.* Gill and Macmillan: London.

Relevant Reports

Conference of Major Religious Superiors (Ireland) (1985) *The Travelling People Today.*

CROSSCARE, (1995) A Report By Kieran KcKeown & Brid McGrath *Accommodating Travelling People.* Dublin

CROSSCARE. (1996) *Celebrating Difference.* An Intercultural

Programme for Senior Primary Classes, Dublin.

Economic and Social Research Institute, 1986, *The Population Structure and Living Circumstance of Irish Travellers: Results from the 1981 Census of Traveller Families*. ESRI, 4 Burlington Rd., Dublin 4.

National Co-ordinating Committee, European Year Against Racism (1997), *Travellers in Ireland, An Examination of Discrimination and Racism*, Irish National co-ordinating Committee for the European Year Against Racism.

The Council for Social Welfare (A Committee of the Catholic Bishops Conference) (1985) *The Travelling People*

Government Reports/Acts

Department of Education (1998) *The Government of Ireland Education Act*. Stationery Office: Dublin.

Department of the Environment (1983) *The Report of the Travelling People Review Body* Stationery Office: Dublin.

Department of the Environment (1995) *The Report of the Task Force on the Travelling Community* Stationery Office: Dublin.

Department of Social Welfare (1963) *The Report of the Commission on Itinerancy* Stationery Office: Dublin.

Southern Health Board. *Woman's Health Consultation Report – The Voice Of Women* (1996)

Publications by the following organisations

The Parish of the Travelling People

In resourcing Traveller faith we have, over the last eight years produced the following

Wrapped in the Mantle of God, (1992) an insight into the faith of the Traveller community expressed through their culture

Do You Know Us At All? J. Hyland (ed), (1993) an educational module about The Traveller Community

First Communion & Penance and Confirmation with accompanying

work book (1994), a culturally appropriate programme for teachers preparing Traveller children, (in particular those out of school who may have missed out on preparation due to their nomadic lifestyle), for the sacraments of First Communion, Reconciliation and Confirmation

The Light Within, (1998) video with study booklet which explores, in a deeper way, the role that faith plays in the day-to-day lives of the Traveller community

Photographic Exhibition (2000) (also entitled *"The Light Within"*), of images of Traveller life and culture with full text and accompanying booklet of photographs and text.

Pre-marriage Video (2000) and accompanying workbook for use with couples from the Traveller community who are planning to get married. The role- plays were developed and acted out by members of the Traveller community.

Later this year we will be publishing a book, exploring the customs and rituals surrounding death in the Traveller community, as a resource for professionals such as nurses, guards, priests and undertakers who are dealing with Travellers at the time of a bereavement.

Pavee Point

Dublin Travellers Education and Development Group (1992) *Irish Travellers: New Analysis and New Initiatives*. Pavee Publications: Dublin.

Nexus Research Co-operative (1994) *Operation of the 1988 Housing Act in Relation to the Accommodation Needs of Travellers* Pavee Point Travellers Centre, 46 North Great Charles St., Dublin 1

Ni Laodhog, N. (ed.) (221995), *A Heritage Ahead: Cultural Action and Travellers*, Pavee Point, Dublin.

O Riain, G. (ed.) (1992), *Traveller Ways, Traveller Words*. Pavee Point, Dublin.

Ryan, L (1998). *Equality Proofing Administrative Procedures*, Pavee Point, Dublin

Pavee Point and the Eastern Health Board (1995) *Primary Health Care for Travellers Project* Pavee Point Travellers' Centre, 46 North

Great Charles St, Dublin 1.

Pavee Point (1993) *Recycling and the Traveller Economy – Income, Jobs, and Wealth Creation*. Pavee Publications: Dublin.

Pavee Publications (1995). *Traveller Accommodation*.

Pavee Publications (1995). *Traveller Inclusion in the Mainstream Labour Force*.

Pavee Publications, (1998), *Bridges to the Future, A Report on Future Roles for the Senior Traveller Training Centres*, Pavee Point, Dublin

Pavee Publication (publication date 2000). *Pavee Pack, a resource pack for teachers of the C.S.P.E. programme in post-primary schools*.

Pavee Point Publications (1997) *Travellers; nomads of Ireland* Dublin.

Speirs, D. *Pavee Pictures*, Pavee Point Publications, Dublin.

Irish Traveller Movement

Irish Traveller Movement (1994) *Still No Place To Go – A Survey on Traveller Accommodation* ITM: Dublin.

Irish Traveller Movement (1994) *Traveller Accommodation and the Law*.

Irish Traveller Movement (1995) *Travellers Learning*.

Irish Traveller Movement (1997) *Travellers and Post-Primary Education* (unpublished). ITM Conference: Limerick.

Videos

Nomadism Now and Then (1991) Pavee Point: Dublin.

Pavee Beoir, Different But Equal. (1999) Pavee Point: Dublin

Pavee Beoir, Her Reproductive Health, (Available 2000), Dublin

Place of Living, Accommodating Travellers (1997) ITM: Dublin.

Pre-Marriage Video (2000) The Parish of the Travelling People: Dublin

The Light Within. (1998) The Parish of the Travelling People: Dublin.

Appendix 7

Contributors

Pat Brady is the liaison officer for accommodation with CROSS-CARE, (the Catholic Social Service Conference of the Dublin Diocese). He has been responsible for the publication of *Accommodating Travelling People* (1996) and *Celebrating Difference* (1996)

Liam Gaul is a native of Wexford town. Liam has a life-long interest in Irish traditional music, song and dance and the various customs and background to this art form. The author wishes to acknowledge R.T.E. and The Long Note Documentary on the life of Johnny Doran for permission to use information in this article, also *Irish Minstrels and Musicians* by Capt. Francis 0'Neill published in 1913.

David Joyce lives in Navan and has been employed by the Irish Traveller Movement since September 1997 as National Accommodation Officer to co-ordinate ITM activities on accommodation.

Mairin Kenny was Principal of St. Kieran's National School, Bray until her retirement last year. Her doctoral thesis *"Routes of Resistance:Travellers and Second –Level Schooling"* was published in 1997. Her article in this book is based on a paper 'Schools, Travellers, Minorities: Where From, Where To?' given by Dr. Kenny at the November 1998 Conference Association of Teachers of Traveller People, and published in the ATTP Journal, *Glocklai* Vol., 2 No. 7/8.

Colm Kilcoyne is parish priest of Cong and Neale in Co. Mayo. He has been very involved in the field of communications and has been, up to recently, a regular columnist with *The Sunday Tribune* and formerly with *The Irish Press*.

Thomas McCann is assistant co-ordinator of, and development worker with, the Irish Traveller Movement. He is a graduate of Maynooth. He has been very active in different Traveller organisations for more than twenty years.

Cathleen McDonagh graduated from All Hallows College with a B.A theology degree and is presently employed by the Co. Dublin V.E.C. as full-time chaplain to the Parish of the Travelling People.

Michael McDonagh is married with five children and lives in a group housing scheme in Navan. He works full-time as a Projects'

Manager for Navan Travellers' Workshops Ltd. He represents Ireland on the World Gypsy Council, and has studied Traveller History and Language for the last 20 years.

Winnie McDonagh lives in Finglas and is married with four children, two boys and two girls. She works as an Education Development Worker with the Traveller Education Project (TESO) in Finglas.

Frank Murphy CM is a member of the Vincentian community. He has been Parish Priest of the Parish of the Travelling People in the Dublin Diocese for the past six years.

Anne O Brien is a catechist with the Co. Dublin VEC and has been working in the Parish of the Travelling People for the past nine years. She is currently editing a book on *The experience of Death and Bereavement in the Traveller Community.*

St. Joseph's Training Centre is in Finglas. Thanks to Fr. Paddy Kelly CssR, who has worked with Travellers for almost twenty years, and to all the Trainees of St. Joseph's who participated in the discussion session of which the article is but a summary. Those quoted were Caroline Collins, Marie Collins, Sandra Collins, Kathleen Lawrence, Brigid Maughan, Geraldine Maughan. Jacqueline McDonagh, Winnie McDonagh, Lisa McDonnell and Pauline McDonnell

Delores O Sullivan lives in Australia where she has lived and worked extensively among the Aboriginal People. She has lectured in Queensland University on the concept of culture with particular reference to its Aboriginal expression. She lived for a time in Dublin and worked with the Traveller community.

Pavee Point, This article is by the Primary Health Care for Travellers Project, which is a partnership between Pavee Point and the Eastern Health Board. We acknowledge all the Travellers who have contributed to and participated in the Primary Health Care for Travellers Project in Pavee Point since its inception in 1994.

Erica Sheehan (editor) is a Graduate of Mater Dei and teaches in Willow Park School. As a member of the Vincentian Volunteers she worked for a year in St. Columba's School Strand St.. For the past five years she has helped in a voluntary capacity in the Parish of the Travelling People. She is currently on a Masters of Education course in Maynooth.